# THE ANALECTS
## OF
## CONFUCIUS

newly translated by  Pyun Yung-tai

directly from the Chinese text

**MINJUNGSUGWAN**

**SEOUL**

**Note:** The Writer is former Prime Minister of the Republic of Korea and presently professor of English at Korea University and the Commercial College of Seoul National University.

# CONTENTS

# CONTENTS

# INTRODUCTION

## 1

This book contains the sayings of Confucius as put down by his followers. But that is not all, though it is, no doubt, the main feature. Descriptions of his doings and habits are found here and there throughout the book. As a matter of fact, an entire chapter is devoted to the meticulous depiction of his personal likes and dislikes, what color he shunned in particular articles of dress, what foods he refused to eat, how he deported himself, even attitudinized, on certain occasions, not excepting situations that elicited his rather piquant humor.

His sayings, too, are often embedded in highly interesting, even pathetic, anecdotes, though they are far more often in the form of dialogue. It is remarkable, however, that most of his imperishable aphorisms stand by themselves, without any background whatsoever. His answers to the same questions, as a rule, vary as the disciples who asked them varied, for he meant them to be specific instructions adapted to the questioning individuals suffering from different weaknesses to be discouraged or lacking different virtues to be strengthened.

It is true that the book also contains, if in a negligible measure, remarks made by certain disciples of Confucius as well as apparently dangling quotations from the ancients who had lived long before he (551∼479 B.C.) was born. Nevertheless they do not jar on the tenor of the book as a whole, for they are largely to supplement the teachings of Confucius.

In short, no other immortal teacher of mankind, not even Socrates, is nearly so well preserved in record as Confucius is in the Analects. In fact, few of our celebrated contemporaries are made so familiar to us as Confucius has been, or rather can be, through this book. If he were still alive and invited to our homes, we should not be at a loss as to how to set him at ease, thanks to the complete knowledge of him and his taste embalmed there.

## 2

There is a tendency to regard Confucianism inalienable from stereotyped manners and rigid formalities. This impression has been created by generations of followers of Confucius who found it always easier and safer to stand pat, so far as ceremonies were concerned, than try to adapt them to the changing environment or use them eclectically. However, an open-minded reading of the Analects of Confucius, disregarding, where necessary, prejudiced commentaries, would help replace this impression with another that Confucius always breathed above the formalities, refusing to be their prisoner. He held them subservient to principles. In response to a question on the essence of rites, he said, "On happy occasions, propriety demands simplicity rather than lavishness; in mourning, sorrowfulness is more becoming than complacency."

On another occasion, he said, "A hemp hat is ritually required, but nowadays one made of pure silk is in vogue. As it is more economical, I will follow the majority. To bow below is the correct manner, but nowadays they bow when they get on to the floor. As it looks discourteous, I will bow below, though it is against the majority." Whatever he uttered invariably indicated rationality, moderation and flexibility.

## 3

Many maintain that Confucianism is nothing but a political philosophy or, at most, a system of morality. Whatever they may say to undervalue it as a religious force, Confucius was essentially a devout and pious man, an implicit believer in the Supreme Being. Only he refrained from talking glibly of the

Divinity, because it seemed to him an outright sacrilege. No man could talk himself into divinity, nor could he talk others into it. By submitting himself to it silently but utterly a man could best induce others to do the same. Confucius hated glibness as intensely as Christ did hypocrisy. Indeed the two evils are allied. There is scarcely any remark of Confucius that does not suggest a silent piety.

Living in a world of multiple spirit-worship, he once boldly announced, "If a man offends Heaven, he has no spirit to pray to." When once advised to make an offering for a recovery from his illness, he answered, "I have already long been praying." He replied curtly to an inquisitive inquirer, "Unable to serve men, how can you serve spirits?" To the same shallow questioner, he again said, "Not knowing life, how can you know death?" He never cast pearls to swine. These remarks cannot be so distorted, as by some, as to argue for his cold agnosticism.

## 4

The Chou Dynasty had long been disintegrating, and, in the days of Confucius, was virtually extinct, with no power whatsoever to control the quarreling and grabbing princes who ruled the numerous splinter nations, large and small, as absolute sovereigns. He flitted from one prince to another like a man utterly without a sense of loyalty. He eagerly tried, and in turn was tried by, one prince after another. He left each, regardless of his own personal comforts, as soon as he found that he could not get anything of real significance done.

This seeming fickleness is understandable only when we comprehend that his loyalty was pledged not to any individual prince but to the entire people of the then known civilized world—the people who had been ruled as one nation with close cultural and moral ties, under the benevolent sage-rulers of the three golden dynasties of Hsia, Yin and Chou, and who might again be united into peace and order as one nation, only if a prince was induced to strike the right moral spark.

In the eyes of Confucius, the whole world was one solid mass of moral combustible, so to speak, awaiting a spark to turn it into a conflagration to consume social vices. A government was where a spark would be most telling. Hence he sought a government service— the only known form of organized social service in his days. Sparking was his mission, preferably in a government but, if that was impossible, anywhere else among his own people.

In brief, he felt he must keep sparking, whether in government or outside of it. Once when he was convinced of a government smothering his spark instead of being sparked by it, he preferred to leave it with that spark still unquenched. He once spoke to his most beloved disciple, Yen Hui, "Only you and I, when accepted, can make the Way of Life the ruling principle of the state and retreat with the uncompromised Truth, when rejected." By retreating he did not mean giving it all up but merely sparking outside a government.

In the view of Confucius, an ordinary citizen could not lead a normal, dutiful life without, in so doing, contributing to good government. Once asked why he did not take part in the government, he replied, "The Book of History comments on filial piety, saying, 'Filial piety alone evokes brotherly love, thus contributing to good government.' Such, too, is participation in government. Why must one get a government position in order to participate in government?"

## 5

Confucius believed that the world should be governed by the wise and the good, that there should be one moral world where all people should ultimately become good and that all working in the government, particularly its leaders, should do so from duty, not for gain. True, he did not go so far as Plato did in his Republic, proposing that the "guardians" be separately brought up with a strict regimen as a distinct class to be devoted to the administration and defense of the nation, having no families of their own, possessing no private property and enjoying everything in common—a sort of collectivized life. Confucius set down, however, stern enough standards for administrators: They must not look for gain; they must set an example themselves in everything; they must elevate the able, making room for them, if necessary; they must not give away positions as favors; they must not practise nepotism.

Both frowned at cupidity in rulers as the arch-evil certain to lead to the ruination of a nation. Their analogy is, however, about to end here. In the case of Confucius, the conception of the state was far more moral and cosmopolitan.

Confucius adored the Sage-Emperors Yao and Shun and extolled them, whenever there was a chance, for their lofty virtues, particularly for the reason that they had stood for succession by ability, not by birth. Shun had served the Emperor Yao nearly a generation, when Yao, recognizing the universal respect and confidence Shun commanded, abdicated in his behalf. Shun likewise abdicated in time for Yü who had long and ably assisted him in administration. Nothing could be more alien to Confucius than nepotism.

One of the commentators, more authoritarian than authoritative, twisted certain passages in the Analects of Confucius so as to harp on nepotism. He may have been nepotic himself and perhaps wanted to make his evil practice look a Confucian tradition. To subordinate private interest to public one is, however, a Confucian precept stressed all through. It is true that Confucianism also enjoins one to be mindful of one's poor relations, but it is made sufficiently clear that that should be done out of one's own pocket. Nothing is further from its teachings than the idea of lavishly favoring one's relations with what are known as political spoils.

Confucius had an occasion to say, "Tsang Won Chung had, in a sense, stolen his position, for he did not invite Liu Hsia Hui to work with him in the government, though he knew that he was abler than himself." Certainly, a man with such a fine sense of honor and public service could not brook so ignoble and pernicious a practice as nepotism.

## 6

Confucius never beat about the bush in pronouncing his judgments. He was extremely direct and plain. He chid his disciples openly and unsparingly. His condemnation had an uplifting effect, however, perhaps because it came from such a wealth of faith that beckoned the person addressed to a higher life. To a powerful government dignitary worrying about stealing, Confucius said, "If you cease to be covetous yourself, the people will not steal, even if encouraged." Could a statement be more direct?

# 7

No great teacher of mankind ever emphasized music more than Confucius. He did not slight physical culture either, though he had few occasions to stress it. Enraptured by a piece of classical music, he was not aware of the flavour of meat three months. He once said, "Poetry arouses a man; manners afford him ground to stand on; music completes him." Terrific stress was laid on learning whenever the subject was up. He said, "The attendant evil of love of good without love of learning is foolishness; that of love of intelligence without love of learning is dissipation; that of love of fidelity without love of learning is disastrousness; that of love of honesty without love of learning is narrowness; that of love of courage without love of learning is violence; that of love of straightness without love of learning is extremeness."

He was ever on the alert to seek for new knowledge. He said, "Mastery of the old and receptivity to the new will qualify a man to be a teacher." It is hard to understand how Confucianism came to be regarded to block the advancement of learning. It is a pity indeed that music, physical culture and sensitivity to new knowledge have been completely atrophied out of the fossilized Confucianism. The fault is not with Confucius, though. Traditions congeal. Organization strangles. What was meant to be the embodiment of a spirit turns out, in the end, to be its grave. Treated as a spirit, Confucius will come to life and move. We have only to polevault to him over the heads of generations of so-called Confucians.

## 8

Some think that Confucianism is synonymous with feudalism and that, therefore, it has been discarded along with other feudal things. This view can not be very right, for Confucianism chiefly deals with man himself rather than his isms. A rounded, well-balanced type of man was needed, of course, to make something even of feudalism. But that type of man is all the more needful now when we suffer from isms more sophisticated but not less baneful. Without this basic stance for the cricket of life, man cannot get any good out of anything; with it, he can make any environment tolerable.

**9**

Confucianism offers mental hygiene we can ill afford to miss. Much as we make of our physical hygiene, we know of no mental hygiene except that psychiatry may have something to do with it. In these times when a seeming government or community curb on those that make a living of destroying the mental health of our youth is decried as a violation of civil rights, Confucius certainly has a message for us. He says, "Do not see an improper thing; do not hear an improper thing; do not say an improper thing; do not do an improper thing." Though we must accept the latter half of the statement logically, at least, what can we do with the first half? What can we see nowadays except "an improper thing?" What can we hear except "an improper thing?" Naturally, therefore, the latter half of the injunction, too, will be just as hard in practice, though accepted for the sake of logic.

## 10

Many label Confucianism as undemocratic because of the remark of Confucius, "The masses can be led but cannot be made to comprehend." In order to evaluate this statement correctly, however, we have to take into consideration what might be termed a sister statement also made by Confucius:- "Men born with understanding are the best; men gaining understanding through learning are next; men who manage to learn after great pains are again next; those that fail to learn even after great pains are the masses and these are the last." So it is clear that Confucius meant the remark only for the people graded lowest in intelligence. By the way, are the masses now even led in the proper sense? The fact is that they are more bamboozled than led in these days.

## 11

The reader will notice that there are insertions. But they are rare on the whole and occur only where, without them, incomprehensibility would result. Otherwise, the original text has not been tampered with in any manner. The sayings of Confucius were

not always arranged chronologically, reminiscences
about a certain dead disciple, for instance, far preceding lamenting utterances on his death. No attempt has
been made, however, to reshuffle them with a view
to giving a more chronological look. Certain passages,
though very few, are placed just like meteorites
are. You see no connection between them and
what surrounds them. Cutting them out would cause
no damage. But they are left. To leave the original
arrangement intact has, at least, the advantage of
making reference to the Chinese text easy for those
readers who might find it interesting to compare
the translation with the original, passage by passage.

## 12

Obscurities have been caused in the Chinese original by misprints and hiatuses accumulated through
the centuries, which, in most cases, we can, at best,
surmise but cannot prove. More numerous obscurities
which happen to be more momentous, too, have
been caused, however, by misinterpretations of commentators. This does not, by any means, imply that
all old commentaries are to be discredited. On the
whole, they are so essential. In fact, many a passage
would not have been made out at all without the
welcome elucidation from a commentator. If the

question were to choose between the total repudiation of all the commentaries and their entire and un-questioned acceptance, the latter would be preferred by any sane person. Nevertheless, it is not safe to assume that they are all infallible. Like other human things, they are not. It is often required that we get free of them, exclusively relying on the text itself. In this way, numerous obscurities have been actually removed in this translation.

## 13

Strictly speaking, no exact equivalent for a word of one language can be found in another, which will be good in all possible combinations or situations. This is doubly true in the case of two languages belonging to different families, such as Chinese and English. For instance, there is no exact English equivalent for the Chinese "chün tzu." There may be English approximations instead, which will do by turns in one context after another but none of which will always make sense, if stuck to in all contexts. "Chün tzu" means "princely man" literally. Some of the English substitutes are "man of virtue", "great man", "man of station", "gentleman", each of which can make more sense than any of the rest in a given context. So with the Chinese word "tao". "A moral view of life", "the Way of Life", "Truth", "principle", "the Way", etc. are possible renditions to be alternately used.

The Chinese word "li", too, requires quite a variety of English terms to cover it in various situations. "Manners", "good manners", "rites", "rituals", "propriety" and "courtesy" are some of them. "Justice" well corresponds to the Chinese "yi" which rather approaches Platonic "justice", though not quite in that concrete sense, implying whatever is right or dictated by reason.

However, the most baffling Chinese word is "jen". It conveys something deeper and broader than any possible English substitute ever can. It comprises the Platonic "wisdom" but it is more than that. It may mean the all-inclusive synthesis of what is human and what is divine in man. Confucius himself never conclusively defined that word. Yet, after all, the only English word capable of stretching so as to approximate it is "good". Jesus once said to a man who had called him good, "Why do you call me good? No one is good except God." Apparently, Jesus used the word in the sense of "Godlike". Confucius seldom pronounced a given man to be good. He always backed away whenever he was asked point-blank whether a certain living person was good, as he would have done, if he had been asked to fall down in worship of him.

## 14

The fact that the present volume consists of twenty chapters would naturally incline the reader to expect as many distinct topics. But definitely that is not the case. The Chinese compiler of the book just happened to find it convenient to make it into twenty tomes. Having no particular subject, each of them had to be distinguished from the rest by a few of its opening words. So has each of the twenty chapters here.

# CHAPTER I

## About Learning

### 1

The Master said, "Is it not gratifying continuously to practise what one has learned? Is one not happy to have a friend come from far-away? Is it not great to be serene in obscurity?"

### 2

Yu Tzu said, "Practising filial piety and reverence to elders, a man is seldom prone to offend his superiors. Not prone to offend superiors, a man never takes to trouble-making.

"A man of virtue concentrates on what is basic. With the base established, the moral view of life will come into being. I say, filial piety and reverence to elders form the basis of being good."

### 3

The Master said, "A man with sweet words and ingratiating manners is seldom good."

**4**

Tseng Tzu said, "I daily question myself on these three points: Do I lack loyalty in acting in behalf of a fellow being? Am I insincere in conversing with a friend? Do I neglect to practise what has been taught me?"

**5**

The Master said, "In ruling a country of one thousand chariots, one should handle affairs reverently so as to inspire the confidence of the people, exercise rigorous economy so as to lighten their burden and use them in their spare time."

**6**

The Master said, "Young men should be devotedly filial at home and reverential abroad, be few in words but faithful in keeping them, love all but associate only with the good. If these practices still leave them some energy, they may apply it to learning."

**7**

Tzu Hsia said, "If a man adores the good to the

point of forgetting women, does his utmost in looking after his parents, forgets himself in the service of his prince and keeps his word in dealing with friends, I will call him cultured, though others may call him ignorant."

## 8

The Master said, "If a scholar fails to deport himself with due gravity, he will forfeit dignity, and, as for his learning, it will lack stability.

"Put loyalty and faithfulness first; associate with no one inferior to yourselves; do not hesitate to repent when wrong."

## 9

Tseng Tzu said, "Let them solemnize their parents' burials and observe commemoration rites for their ancestors and the people will be more kindly disposed toward one another."

## 10

Tzu Ts'in said to Tzu Kung, "Now that the Master has come to this country, he must wish to be informed of the political situation here. Will he seek it or wait till it is given?"

Tzu Kung said, "Mild, meek, pious and plain, the Master gets by yielding. His way of seeking is quite different from that of others."

## 11

The Master said, "A man's intentions are to be watched during his father's lifetime and his conducts after his demise. He who preserves his father's ways intact for three years from his death can be called filial."

## 12

Yu Tzu said, "In the application of rules of manners, harmony is to be valued. The ways, great and small, of Ancient Kings all had harmony as their key.

"The skipping of certain rules is done on the basis of harmony, which, in turn, cannot be allowed to wander unbounded by rules at all."

## 13

Yu Tzu said, "A pledge not straying from reason will be easily kept; a show of respect not straying from prescribed rules of manners will never incur shame or disgrace; an association not ignoring one's own kind will remain honorable. "

## 14

The Master said, "If a scholar eats without seeking satiety and takes a house without hankering after ease, if he is quick in practice but slow of speech and if, above all, he takes himself to one with superior moral insight for rectification, he can indeed be said to be fond of learning. "

## 15

Tzu Kung once asked, "What do you think of a person who, though poor, is not given to cringing or who, though rich, is not overbearing?"

The Master replied, "Good, but not to compare with one who is happy in poverty or who, for all his riches, relishes propriety. "

Tzu Kung then said, "The Book of Poems says, 'Like grinding on top of cutting; like polishing on top of chiselling.' Does it not describe something like that?"

The Master said, "You are qualified to discuss Poems. Told what precedes, you know what will follow."

# 16

The Master said, "A man need not be concerned about men not knowing him; he should be concerned about his not knowing men."

# CHAPTER II

## To Rule by Morals...

### 1

The Master said, "To rule by morals is like the loadstar, lying where it does, attracting all the other stars to face towards it."

### 2

The Master said, "The three hundred poems can be summarized as ingenuous expressions."

### 3

The Master said, "When the people are marshalled by administration and uniformalized by a penal system, they may escape punishment but will remain shameless.

"When they are led with morals and uniformalized with good manners, they will have sense of shame and moral consciousness as well."

### 4

The Master said, "At fifteen, my attention turned

to learning; at thirty, my purpose in life got set; at forty, I was free from temptations; at fifty, I learned how to resign myself to Providence; at sixty, what came through the ear could not disturb my inner peace; at seventy, I did what my heart listed and yet never went wrong."

## 5

Asked by Meng Yi Tzu how one could be filial, the Master said, "No contravention."

While Fan Ts'u was driving the carriage, the Master said, "As Meng Sun(the personal name of Meng Yi Tzu) asked me about filial piety, I said, 'No contravention.'"

Fan Ts'u asked, "What do you mean by that?" The Master replied, "One should serve one's father with proper manners, in his life, bury him with proper rites when he dies, and hold the annual memorial service for him with proper rites."

## 6

Asked by Meng Wu Po on filial piety, the Master said, "What worries parents most is their son's ill health."

## 7

At Tzu Yu's inquiry about filial piety, the Master

said, "In these days, filial piety is regarded fulfilled when support is given the parents. Aren't even dogs and horses fed? Without paying them reverence, how can you differentiate between them and domestic animals?"

## 8

Asked by Tzu Hsia on filial piety, the Master said, "Genuine expression of reverence is what is difficult. Something having to be done, the son does it for the old man; when there are food and drink, he sees that the old man is served first. Could this be the sum total of filial piety?"

## 9

The Master said, "When I talk to Hui, he is submissive a whole day, saying only yea like a fool. When alone, however, he does self-searching unceasingly until he makes out the meaning of what he heard. Hui is no fool indeed!"

## 10

The Master said, "See the means a man employs, scrutinize his motivation, observe what gives him comfort and he will no longer be able to conceal himself."

## 11

The Master said, "Mastery of the old and receptivity to the new will qualify a man to be a teacher."

## 12

The Master said, "A man of virtue is not made to a function."

## 13

Requested by Tzu Kung to define a man of virtue, the Master said, "He is a man to practise first and say afterwards."

## 14

The Master said, "A man of virtue is universal-minded, not selfishly biased; a small man is selfishly biased, not universal-minded."

## 15

The Master said, "Learning without thinking is confusing; thinking without learning is perilous."

# 16

The Master said, "Studying heretic views does nothing but harm."

# 17

The Master said, "Yu, shall I tell you what knowing is? When you know, say you do and when you do not know, say you don't. That is knowing."

# 18

Tzu Chang was engaged in learning for emolument. The Master said, "If you screen out the doubtful from all you hear and express the rest carefully, you will make few mistakes; if you screen out the dangerous from all you see and practise the rest carefully, you will have little to repent. If you have few mistakes in speech and little to repent in conduct, emolument will come of itself."

# 19

Prince Ai Kung asked, "What shall we do to make the people obedient?"

The Master replied, "If you raise the upright and

leave the crooked, the people will obey; if you raise the crooked and leave the upright, they will not obey. "

## 20

Chi K'ang Tzu inquired, "What is the way to make the people respectful, loyal and industrious?"

The Master answered, "Dealing with them with dignity will inspire respect; filial piety and paternal love will inspire loyalty; promoting the able and instructing the inept will make them industrious. "

## 21

Someone said to Confucius, "Why don't you take part in government?"

The Master replied, "The Book of History comments on filial piety, saying, 'Filial piety alone evokes brotherly love, thus contributing to good government.' Such, too, is participation in government. Why must one get a government position in order to participate in government?"

## 22

The Master said, "A man lacking reliability is

utterly useless. How can vehicles, large or small, move without the yoke-piece?"

## 23

Tzu Chang inquired the possibility of knowing things ten generations away.

The Master explained, "The manners of the Yin Dynasty were based on those of the Hsia Dynasty, and certain deletions and additions are traceable. The manners of the Chou Dynasty were likewise based on those of the Yin Dynasty, and certain deletions and additions are traceable. If there should be dynasties that would succeed to the Chou Dynasty, things even a hundred generations off could be anticipated."

## 24

The Master said, "A man who goes beyond his station and makes offerings to a spirit not properly his own commits flattery.

"A man who sees a right thing to do but does not do it is a coward."

# CHAPTER III
## Eight Rows of Dancers···

### 1

Commenting on Chi's (a minister of the kingdom of Lu) employing eight rows of eight dancers each at his family rite, proper only for a king, the Master said, "If this is tolerable, what is not tolerable?"

### 2

The houses of Prince Huan Kung's three mistresses had the practice of clearing their sacrificial foods away to the music called Yung. The Master commenting said, "The music says in part, 'Whilst the princes assist at the rite, gravely majestic is the Emperor.' How dare they arrogate this description to themselves?"

### 3

The Master said, "If a man is not good, what has he to do with good manners? Again, what has he to do with music?"

**4**

Lin Fang inquired what was the essence of good manners.

The Master said, "Great indeed is your question." "On happy occasions," he continued, "propriety demands simplicity rather than lavishness; in mourning, sorrowfulness is more becoming than complacency."

**5**

The Master said, "Barbarian tribes under a prince are worse off than princeless peoples of the Middle Kingdom."

**6**

Chi was going to offer a sacrifice on T'aisan, a mountain outside his own realm, a thing ritually forbidden. The Master asked Jan Yu, his chief minister, "Can you not dissuade him from it?" He replied, "No, I cannot." The Master said, "Oh dear! Can you say that T'aisan is less discerning than Lin Fang in the matter of propriety?"

**7**

The Master said, "A man of virtue contends in

nothing. If there is anything requiring his contention, it must be archery. He steps on the shooting platform after bowing and showing deference. When defeated, he gets down and drinks for punishment. In this way, his contention, too, is of a virtuous man. "

## 8

Tzu Hsia asked the meaning of the old poem saying, "How comely are the arch smiles and how fair and clear the eyes! Embellishment is to lie on plain substance. "

The Master answered, "Painting must follow a plain background. "

"Are manners what follows, then?"

The Master said, "It is you that give me a lift. You are indeed qualified to discuss Poems. "

## 9

The Master said, "I can discourse about the rites of the Hsia Dynasty but those of the Kingdom of Ki(a tributary of Hsia towards its end) are not demonstrable. I can discourse about the rites of the Yin Dynasty but those of the Kingdom of Sung (a tributary of Yin towards its end) are not demonstrable. It is because of insufficiency of records, written or oral. If there were sufficient records, I could demonstrate them. "

## 10

The Master said, "In regard to the great quinquennial memorial service of the royal household, I am irked to observe the proceedings that follow the libation for evocation. " (For by then the officiants grew lax.)

## 11

In response to someone seeking for the full explanation of the quinquennial memorial service of the royal household, the Master said, "I do not know much. To one who does, ruling the world would be as easy as showing this." So saying, he pointed to his palm.

## 12

At his ancestral memorial services, the Master conducted himself as if the spirits of his forebears were present. In offering sacrifices to spirits other than ancestral, he likewise behaved as if those spirits were present right there.

The Master said, "If I do not personally participate in a service, for me, at least, there exists no service."

## 13

Wang Sun Chia, a minister of the Kingdom of Wei, asked, "There is a saying, 'One should rather please the kitchen spirit than the household tutelary spirit.' What does it mean?" (He suggested thereby that, to gain political influence, Confucius had better curry favor with him instead of the Prince.)

The Master answered, "There is nothing in it. If a man offends Heaven, he has no spirit to pray to."

## 14

The Master said, "Benefiting from the two preceding dynasties, Chou is culturally great. I will follow Chou's ways."

## 15

At the shrine of Chou Kung, the founding prince of Lu, the Master made a point of inquiring about everything.

Someone said, "Who says that this man from Chou County is well versed in rites? He always asks questions at the royal shrine."

Hearing it, the Master said, "That is exactly what the rites demand."

## 16

The Master said, "An ancient rule in archery says that it is of no consequence whether the target leather is pierced through, if it is hit at all, for allowances must be made for the inequality in men's physical force."

## 17

Tzu Kung wanted, for economy, to save the sheep from the monthly offering by his prince announcing to his ancestors the commencement of each new month, which, now grown so perfunctory, the prince himself had long ceased to attend.

The Master said to Tzu Kung, "Do you want to spare the sheep? I want to spare the rite."

## 18

The Master said, "When I serve the Prince with all the prescribed manners, people say I am fawning."

## 19

Prince Ting Kung inquired the proper way for the prince to use his subjects and for the subjects to serve their prince.

Confucius answered, "The prince is to use his subjects with courtesy; the subjects are to serve their prince with loyalty."

## 20

The Master said, "The Poem titled Kuan Chü depicts pleasure without lust and sorrow without despair."

## 21

Consulted by Prince Ai Kung on the establishment of a new temple to be dedicated to the God of Earth, replacing the burnt one, Tzai Wo said, "The Hsia Dynasty planted pines all over the place, Yin nut-bearing pines and Chou chestnut trees to drive fear into the people, it is said." (The Chinese word for chestnut is homophonous with that for trembling.)

Upon hearing this, the Master said, "It is of no use to criticize a thing already done or try to dissuade from what is already set or blame what is past."

## 22

The Master said, "Kuan Chung is a man of small caliber."

Someone asked, "Was Kuan Chung parsimonious?"

"He had a triple-terraced mansion and none of his household servitors had to do double duties. So he can not have been parsimonious."

"Did Kuan Chung, then, know manners?"

"His prince built a screen wall behind the gate and Kuan Chung also had one built. His prince had a stand to put drained wine cups on when feasting with a guest prince and Kuan Chung likewise had one. If he knew manners, who does not?"

## 23

The Master said to the Grand Master of Music of Lu, "Music is not hard to understand. At the start, the sounds of all the instruments break forth simultaneously. Then they merge into grand harmony, still severally discernible, and weave on like so many endless rhythmic sonic strands to the completion of the piece."

## 24

In Yi, the frontier guard sought an interview,

saying, "When a great man came here, I never failed to pay him my respects." One of the followers conducted him to Confucius. On coming out, he said, "Why should you feel grieved, friends, at his failure to get an influential government position? The world has been too long in chaos. Heaven is going to make the Master a wooden gong for awakening."

## 25

Commenting on the Emperor Shun's music, the Master said, "It is all beautiful and all good." But he said on the music of King Wu, the Conqueror, "It is all beautiful but not all good."

## 26

The Master said, "If a man is not generous when wielding power, fails to deport himself respectfully and shows no grief in mourning, I need not be any longer bothered about his worth."

# CHAPTER IV

## To Live Among the Good...

### 1

The Master said, "It is edifying to live among the good. If a man fails to choose good neighbors, how can he be regarded wise?"

### 2

The Master said, "A man who is not good cannot long live in poverty contentedly, nor can he long enjoy prosperity. The good delight in goodness, while the wise utilize it."

### 3

The Master said, "A good man alone can love or hate a fellow being."

### 4

The Master said, "If a man is intent on goodness, he will avoid evil."

## 5

The Master said, "Though wealth and position are what people want, they must be given up, if they cannot be retained honorably. Though poverty and lowliness are what people dislike, they must not be shunned, unless they can be avoided honorably. Running away from goodness, how can a man of virtue maintain his honor? He never lets goodness go even for a moment. He clings to it even in unguarded moments, even in upsetting surprises."

## 6

The Master said, "I am yet to see a lover of good or a hater of evil. A lover of good loves nothing better, while a hater of evil is good himself in that he never lets an evil-doer have anything to do with his own person.

"Suppose a man could devote one single day to goodness. I never saw any person fail because of insufficient strength.

"There may have been such people. Then, I have just never met them."

## 7

The Master said, "Men commit faults according

to their kind. A fault reveals how good a man is. "

## 8

The Master said, "Let a man hear the Truth in the morning and he may die in the evening without regret. "

## 9

The Master said, "A scholar who is intent on seeking the Truth and yet ashamed of poor clothing and feeding is not good enough to talk with. "

## 10

The Master said, "In his behavior in the world, a man of virtue has nothing he is pre-determined to do or not to do. His only test for everything is whether it is right. "

## 11

The Master said, "Great men cherish virtues, whereas small men cherish comforts. Great men mind justice, whereas small men mind favors. "

## 12

The Master said, "Fling yourselves about as selfish interest dictates and you will make many enemies."

## 13

The Master said, "If a man can rule the country with courtesy and humility, he will have no difficulty; if he cannot, his understanding of courtesy is doubtful."

## 14

The Master said, "Do not be downcast because you get no position; rather be anxious about how to acquit yourselves creditably when you get one. Do not be downcast because people do not know you; rather seek to be worthy to be known."

## 15

The Master said, "Ts'an (Tseng Tzu's personal name), remember, my Way of Life consists of one single all-pervading principle." Tseng Tzu said yea.

When the Master retired and his followers inquired what it meant, Tseng Tzu said, "The Master's principle is nothing but sincerity and sympathy."

## 16

The Master said, "What moves a great man is justice, but a small man is moved by interest."

## 17

The Master said, "Strive to match the good when noticed in people; do a self-searching when faults are found in them."

## 18

The Master said, "When you have to remonstrate with your parents, do so in a diffident, roundabout way. Though your advice goes unheeded, revere and obey them all the more; unappreciated toil should not lead you to grumbling."

## 19

The Master said, "When parents are with you,

do not go out too far. When you go out, it must be to places known to them."

## 20

The Master said, "One must take note of one's parents' ages, partly for joy to see them live long and partly from dread of their approaching end."

## 21

The Master said, "Ancients did not lightly speak their minds lest their actions should fail to be up to the mark."

## 22

The Master said, "One seldom errs by simplicity."

## 23

The Master said, "A man of virtue is inclined to be slow of speech but quick in practice."

## 24

The Master said, "The virtuous are never lonely.

They are bound to have friends."

## 25

Tzu Yu said, "Advising a prince too often only invites disfavor and advising a friend too often estrangement."

# CHAPTER V
## Kung Yeh Ch'ang···

### 1

Declaring that Kung Yeh Ch'ang would make a good husband, his incarceration not having been caused by any real crime on his part, the Master married his own daughter to him.

### 2

Saying that Nan Jung was a man to rise in a well-ordered world and avoid punishment, at least, in a disordered one, the Master gave his elder brother's daughter away to him.

### 3

With regard to Tzu Chien, the Master said, "How virtuous this man is! If there are no men of virtue in Lu, from whom did he learn all these virtues?"

### 4

Tzu Kung asked, "What do you think I am?"

The Master answered, "You are a vessel."

"What vessel?"

"A sacrificial vessel of quality."

## 5

Someone said, "Yung is good and not oily."

The Master said, "No, he is not oily. Dealing with people outspokenly, he is often hated. Though I do not know that he is a good man, certainly he is not oily."

## 6

Advised by Confucius to enter government service, Ch'i-tiao K'ai said, "I am not so confident that I can do it well." The Master was pleased.

## 7

The Master said, "Though, my teachings gone unheeded, I get away on a raft to the sea, it is Yu that will follow me even there." Tzu Lu (Yu's pen name) exulted to hear it.

The Master said, "Yu is far more daring than I am. I have no use for him."

## 8

Meng Wu Po asked if Tzu Lu was good. The Master said, "I do not know." Asked again, the Master said, "Tzu Lu can be put in charge of the army in a nation of one thousand chariots. But I do not know if he is good."

Asked how Ch'iu was, the Master said, "He can be made a steward in a town of one thousand houses or in a nobleman's household of one hundred chariots. But I do not know if he is good."

Asked how Ch'ih was, the Master said, "He will acquit himself well, if made to converse, in full dress, with foreign envoys at Court. But I do not know if he is good."

## 9

The Master asked Tzu Kung, "Who is better, you or Hui?"

Tzu Kung replied, "How could I hope to match Hui? Hearing one, he knows ten. Hearing one, I know only two."

The Master said, "You cannot well compare with him. I fully agree with you there."

# 10

Tsai Yü stayed in bed sleeping in the daytime. The Master said, "Rotten wood cannot be carved; a wall built of dirty earth cannot be embellished. Why should I blame you at all?"

The Master said, "Formerly I used to judge people by hearing what they professed and taking their practice for granted, but now I judge people by hearing what they profess and watching their practice, too. This change is due to Tsai Yü."

# 11

The Master said, "I am yet to see a straight man." Someone answered, "Well, there is Shen Ch'ang." The Master retorted, "Ch'ang is covetous and so how can he be straight?"

# 12

Tzu Kung said, "I do not want people to interfere with me, nor do I wish to interfere with them." The Master said, "It is just beyond you."

# 13

Tzu Kung said, "We can learn about the Master's

manners and culture, but we never hear him discourse on human nature or Providence."

## 14

Aware that he failed to act out all that he was reputed to be capable of, Tzu Lu came to dread repute itself.

## 15

Tzu Kung asked, "Why is the word 'won' included in the name, K'ang Won Tzu?"

The Master said, "Because he is nimble of mind and fond of learning, thinking it not beneath himself even to ask his inferiors for information, his name carries the epithet (meaning 'culture')."

## 16

The Master said, "Tzu Ch'an possesses four gentlemanly traits: He conducts himself with humility, serves his superiors with respect, looks after the people with munificence and employs them with justice."

# 17

The Master said, "Yen P'ing Chung indeed knows the art of keeping friends. He never slackens in respecting them."

# 18

The Master said, "Tsang Won Chung keeps a large tortoise for a mascot in an exclusive edifice, on whose capitals of pillars and inter-beam props mountains and aquatic plants are carved respectively. How can he be termed intelligent?"

# 19

Tzu Chang said, "Tzu Won became Premier three times but he did not show pleasure even once. He was dismissed three times but he did not show displeasure any time. Besides, he never failed to tell his successor what he had been doing. What do you think of him?"

The Master answered, "He was dutiful."

"Was he not good?"

"I do not know. It may be too much to call him good."

"When Ts'ui Tzu assassinated his own prince of

Ch'i, Ch'en Won Tzu, avoiding him, went to another country, leaving forty horses he owned. Soon he went to still another country, saying that the officials there were of the same sort as Ts'ui Tzu. Yet this soon repeated itself once more. What would you say of him?"

The Master said, "He was clean."

"Was he not good?"

"I do not know. It may be too much to call him good, though."

## 20

Chi Won Tzu thought three times before he acted. Hearing this, the Master said, "It is enough to think twice."

## 21

The Master said, "Ning Wu Tzu showed intelligence in a well-ordered world, but he acted like a fool in a disordered one. Though his intelligence is reachable, his foolishness is beyond reach."

## 22

In the midst of privations in Ch'en, the Master

said, "Let us go home and at once. Our young ones left there are getting at once extreme and simple. They are lavish in expression and do not know how to restrain."

## 23

The Master said, "Po Yi and Shu Ch'i never remembered old evils in people and consequently made few enemies."

## 24

The Master said, "Who said that Wei Sheng Kao was straight? When someone asked vinegar of him, he borrowed some from his neighbor and gave it to him."

## 25

The Master said, "Tso Ch'iu Ming is ashamed of sweet words, obsequious manners and excessive humility; so am I. He is ashamed to feign friendliness to a person, against whom he harbors a grudge; so am I."

## 26

The Master once said to Yen Yüan and Chi Lu

who were with him, "How about speaking out your wishes?"

Tzu Lu (another name of Chi Lu) said, "I wish I had carriages and costly fur coats so that I could unstintingly share them with my friends."

Yen Yüan (another name of Yen Hui)said, "I wish not to display good and not to show toil."

Tzu Lu said to Confucius, "We wish to hear your wishes, too."

The Master responded, "I wish to comfort the old, be faithful to friends and cherish the young."

## 27

The Master said, "Alack! I have never seen a man find himself in the wrong and internally arraign himself."

## 28

The Master said, "Even a hamlet of a dozen houses is not without a person as sincere and faithful as I, but not always does it have one as full of passion for learning."

# CHAPTER VI
## Yung...

### 1

The Master said, "Yung has the making of a ruler."

Chung Kung (the pen name of Yung) asking how Tzu Shang Po Tzu was, the Master said, "Acceptable, for he is gifted with simplicity."

Chung Kung again queried, "Is it not enough that a ruler, while living in a dignified manner, deals with his people with simplicity? Is it not rather too much to live, too, in so simple a way as to lose dignity, besides acting simply?"

The Master said, "You have said right."

### 2

When Prince Ai Kung asked Confucius which of his disciples was most devoted to learning, the Master answered, "There was one Yen Hui very eager to learn. He let no anger drift to a third person; he never committed the same fault twice. Unfortunately he died young and is no more. There is none other so fond of learning that I know of."

## 3

Tzu Hua gone to Ch'i as envoy, Jan Tzu asked grain for his mother. The Master said, "Give her three bushels." Asked for more, he said, "Give her eight bushels then." Jan Tzu gave her, however, many times as much.

The Master said, "Ch'ih(Tzu Hua's personal name) went to Ch'i drawn by sleek horses and clad in costly fur dress. I hear that a man of virtue helps people just to enable them to tide over a difficulty, not to make them richer."

## 4

When Wüan Ssu was made a magistrate, he refused to take his salary of grain as too much.

The Master said to him, "Why, have you no poor neighbors and relations to help?"

## 5

The Master said about Chung Kung(of mean birth), "If a streaked cow's (unfit for sacrifice) youngling is flaming red in skin and regular of horns, will the spirits of the mountains and rivers leave it, even though people making offerings do not wish to use it?"

# 6

The Master said, "Hui never strays from goodness—not for three long months. With the rest, the arrival of a new day or moon marks the end."

# 7

When Chi K'ang Tzu asked whether Chung Yu was fit for administration, the Master said, "As he is courageous, he can be helpful, of course." Asked whether Tz'u was fit, the Master said, "As he is a man of the world in a good sense, he will be, of course, useful in administration." Asked the same about Ch'iu, the Master said, "Why, of course, for he is versatile."

# 8

When Chi sent for Min Tzu Ch'ien to make him magistrate of Pi, Min said to the messenger, "Please be so good as to apologize for me. But, if you come again for it, I shall be over the boundary river Wun."

# 9

Po Niu was ill and the Master paid him a visit.

Holding the ailing man's hand through the window, the Master said, "Impossible! This is fate! To think of such a man being stricken with this disease!"

## 10

The Master said, "How pure-minded Hui is! Living in a hovel, taking a little rice and water for his usual meal, an intolerable condition to live in, he is always happy. How pure-minded Hui is indeed!"

## 11

Jan Ch'iu said to Confucius, "Not that I dislike what you teach, but I have not enough strength to carry it out." The Master said, "A man short of strength usually stops halfway exhausted. But now you are determined not to start at all."

## 12

The Master exhorted Tzu Hsia, saying, "Be a cultured man of moral greatness; do not be one with moral meanness."

## 13

The Master asked Tzu Yu, the magistrate of Wu

Ch'eng, "Have you found any able man?" He answered, "There is one T'an T'ai Mieh Ming. He always walks on roads, shunning narrow short cuts; he never comes to my room except on matters of public concern."

## 14

The Master said, "Meng Chih Fan was truly modest. He brought up the rear in a retreat. About to enter the city gate, he whipped his horse, saying, 'I am not deliberately in the rear, looking so brave. It is this slow horse.'"

## 15

The Master said, "Unless gifted with the artful tongue of Ceremony Master T'o and the handsomeness of Prince Ts'ao of Sung, one can hardly get on in these days."

## 16

The Master said, "Who can go out without passing through the door? Then why do they evade this Way of Life?"

# 17

The Master said, "Virtue outbalancing learning makes a man boorish, while learning outbalancing virtue makes him shallow. These two blended into harmony alone make a great man."

# 18

The Master said, "Man is born of one straight simple principle. To be confused out of it and yet **live** on is just fortuitous."

# 19

The Master said, "To perceive the Truth cannot compare with liking it. To like it cannot compare with being happy in it."

# 20

The Master said, "With men above the average higher things can be discussed, but to those below it they must not be mentioned."

# 21

When Fan Ts'u asked what wisdom was, the

Master said, "To stress what the people ought to do and regard spirits with reverence, not with familiarity, may be called wise. "

Asked what goodness was, the Master answered, "To attend to what is urgent before you think of gain may be called good. "

## 22

The Master said, "The wise delight in water, while the good delight in mountains. The wise are mercurial but the good are serene. The wise are elated but the good are stable. "

## 23

The Master said, "Ch'i reformed will become Lu; Lu reformed will become the Ideal State. "

## 24

The Master said, "If an angled bottle loses angles, can it still be called an angled bottle?"

## 25

Tsai Wo asked, "Will a good man plunge into a

well, if told that a man is fallen there?"

The Master answered, "How could that be? A good man may be led but cannot be made to fall; he can be cheated but cannot be confused."

## 26

The Master said, "If a man of virtue learn and read as widely as possible but keep within the bounds of established manners, he may not be far from the Way of Life."

## 27

Out of regard for etiquette, Confucius visited Nan Tzu, the unchaste wife of the Prince of Wei, at her own invitation, and Tzu Lu showed displeasure.

The Master protested vowing, "If I did wrong, Heaven will forsake me. Heaven, I repeat, will forsake me."

## 28

The Master said, "The Golden Mean is a consummate virtue. The average man seldom keeps it long."

## 29

Tzu Kung said, "If a man does things that benefit the masses and relieves multitudes in distress, what is your opinion of him? Can he be called good?"

The Master answered, "Why is one to make a business of goodness? What one should strive after is holiness. Yao and Shun, too, felt they were short of that.

"A good man, you know, wishing to stand himself, helps others stand, and, wishing to prosper himself, helps others prosper.

"Thus to make oneself the criterion to decide what to do to others may be called the means of being good."

# CHAPTER VII

## Compilation...

### 1

The Master said, "In confining writing to compilation instead of producing creative works and trusting and loving ancient literatures, I presumptuously compare myself with my dear Lao P'eng."

### 2

The Master said, "Perceiving through reflection, seeking the Truth without fatigue, teaching others untiringly, these are no burden on me."

### 3

The Master said, "To neglect practising virtues, to fail to pursue a study to the finish, inability to follow what right I perceive, inability to reform faults, these are my worries."

### 4

The Master was relaxed and genial when he was at home.

## 5

The Master said, "Senility has progressed in me so alarmingly. It is long since I ceased dreaming about Prince Chou Kung (his paragon of virtue)."

## 6

The Master said, "Let seeking the Truth be our aim.

"Let virtues control our actions.

"Let goodness be the fountainhead of our motivation.

"Let art give play to our mind."

## 7

The Master said, "I never refused to teach anyone who came to learn, bringing dried meat as a token of respect."

## 8

The Master said, "I do not teach those who show no passion for learning, nor do I prompt those who are not anxious to express. Suppose I raise a corner of a subject, so to speak, and no response is shown by

the learner as by the other three corners in the case
of a box, I do not further develop the subject. "

## 9

The Master never ate to the full by the side of
the bereaved.

He never sang on the same day that he cried for
mourning.

## 10

The Master said to Yen Wüan, "Only you and I,
when accepted, can make the Way of Life the ruling
principle of the state and retreat with the uncompromised Truth, when rejected. "

Tzu Lu asked, "Whom would you have with you
in marshalling a great army?"

The Master replied, "I would not have a man who
will die without regret, fighting a tiger barehanded
or wading a river. One who is careful, facing a
situation, and succeeds in an enterprise through
good planning would have to be my choice. "

## 11

The Master said, "If it were given me to be rich,

4

I would even make myself a whip-wielding lackey.
Otherwise, I would just do what I pleased."

## 12

What taxed the Master's attention most were
purification, warfare and disease.

## 13

In Ch'i the Master heard the famed music attrib-
uted to the Sage-Emperor Shun. Enraptured by it,
he was not aware of the flavour of meat three
months. He remarked, "I never thought music
could be so enchanting."

## 14

Jan Yu asked, "Is the Master for the accession of
the Prince of Wei?" Tzu Kung answered, "Good, I
will ask him."

Tzu Kung came to Confucius and asked, "What
manner of men were Po Yi and Shu Ch'i?"

"They were ancient men of virtue."

"Did they complain (encountering hardships after
their flight from the country)?"

"They sought what they thought was good and got

it. Why should they have complained?"

Tzu Kung came out and said, "The Master is not for the Prince."

# 15

The Master said, "Eating poor rice, drinking only water and having the bended elbow for a pillow, a man can still keep his inner peace.

"Getting wealth and position through crooked means is no more significant to me than a fleeting cloud overhead."

# 16

The Master said, "If Heaven grant me a few more years so as to complete the study of the Book of Changes, I may, at least, be free from blunders."

# 17

The Master's perennial sources of exhortation were the Book of Poems, the Book of History and practical manners and rites.

# 18

When Shen Chu Liang asked Tzu Lu about Confucius, he did not reply.

The Master said, "Why did you not say that I am so enthusiastic as to neglect food, so blissful as to forget worries and thus utterly oblivious of the approaching senility?"

## 19

The Master said, "I am not born wise. I only love the ways of the ancients and assiduously seek after the Truth."

## 20

The Master never mentioned prodigies, superhuman feats of strength, incidents of violence and spirits.

## 21

The Master said, "When I walk with two men, either is bound to be my teacher. I choose the good one and make him my model; I detect the bad one for my own reform."

## 22

The Master said, "Heaven has reposed the Truth

in me. What harm, then, can Huan T'ui (who had just tried to kill Confucius) do to me?"

## 23

The Master said to his disciples, "Do you think I have some secrets that you are not let into? Truly I keep nothing from you. I do nothing without your knowing all about it."

## 24

The Master employed four categories of instruction, namely, culture, behavior, loyalty and faithfulness.

## 25

The Master said, "I know I cannot hope to see a sage. I shall be contented with meeting a man of virtue."

The Master said, "I know I cannot hope to see a good man. I shall be contented to meet a steady man.

"One who pretends to have when he has not, to be full when empty, to be great when puny, can hardly make a steady man."

# 26

The Master angled, never netted, fish; he never darted sleeping game.

# 27

The Master said, "There are people who act or say a thing without making sure of its rightness. Certainly I am not that sort. To cull the good from the much one hears and practise it, and see much and learn to discern is next to born wisdom."

# 28

A boy from Hu Hsiang whose inhabitants were regarded cultural outcasts was granted an interview, and the followers were perplexed.

The Master said, "If a man comes reformed, we have to accept his reformation, heedless of his evil past. When he comes forward, we have to let him and need not concern ourselves about his possible slipping back. Why should we single this boy out for harsh treatment?"

# 29

The Master said, "Is goodness far off? The moment a man desires it, it arrives."

## 30

When Ch'en Ssu Pai inquired if Prince Shao Kung knew manners, the Master said, "Yes, he does."

When Confucius was away, Ch'en beckoned to Wu Ma Ch'i and said, "I hear, a man of virtue is not partial. Is he, too, partial sometimes? Prince Shao Kung married a girl of the same family name as his and manipulated her name to cover up the shameful fact. If he knows manners, who does not?"

When informed of it by Wu Ma Ch'i, the Master said, "I am fortunate. When I am in the wrong, people all know it."

## 31

Singing with a friend, the Master always made him sing the song once more, if he was thought to have sung it well. Then he sang it himself.

## 32

The Master said, "I can keep abreast of people in cultural things. As for sterling character putting virtues into practice, I have none of it."

## 33

The Master said, "How dare I claim to be holy or good? I may be said rather to strive tirelessly after these ideals and teach men without fatigue toward the same." Kung Hsi Hua said, "That is exactly where your pupils fail."

## 34

The Master fell ill and Tzu Lu asked him to pray for his recovery. The Master asked, "Is there a way?" Tzu Lu answered, "Yes. An old memorial writing says, 'Pray ye to Heaven and Earth.'" The Master said, "I have already long been praying."

## 35

The Master said, "Extravagance leads to insolence, while frugality to drabness. I would rather have drabness than insolence, though."

## 36

The Master said, "Great men are always expansive, while small men are always worrying."

# 37

The Master was mild yet solemn, dignified yet not fearful, humble yet easeful.

# CHAPTER VIII

## T'ai Po...

### 1

The Master said, "T'ai Po may indeed be said to have been supremely virtuous. He thrice relinquished his legitimate claims to the throne. But he did it in such an unnoticeable way that the people did not know it at all, far from praising him for it."

### 2

The Master said, "Humility without manners results in toil; caution without manners in timidity; daring without manners in violence; honesty without manners in intolerance."

### 3

Tseng Tzu said, "Regard for kin by men of station would encourage the people to be good. Leaving no old assistant cold outside would make them kindly."

### 4

Falling ill for the last time, Tseng Tzu called his

disciples to his side and said, "Open and see my hands and feet. A poem says, 'Cautious and watchful as if on the brink of an abyss or treading on thin ice.' My little friends, now I know that I have escaped harm."

## 5

When Tseng Tzu fell ill, Meng Ching Tzu visited him.

Tseng Tzu said, "A dying bird chirps plaintively; a dying man leaves a kind word.

"A man of station should value three points most out of the mass of wisdom he has garnered. His conduct should be neither impetuous nor sluggish; his countenance should look earnest and reliable; his utterance should be far from vulgar or cynical. As to detailed matters, they could be left to assistants."

## 6

Tseng Tzu said, reminiscing about Yen Hui, "These were the practices of my friend. Gifted, he asked the ungifted questions. Having much himself, he asked those having little for information. Rich, he acted as if he were poor; full, he pretended to be empty. Insulted, he did not retaliate."

## 7

Tseng Tzu said, "Entrusted with the care of a child prince and put in charge of a realm a hundred *li* wide, suppose a man does not waver in his loyalty in a crisis, is he a virtuous man? Yes, he is indeed."

## 8

Tseng Tzu said, "A dedicated man must possess a large heart and great fortitude, for his responsibility is heavy and his way far.

"Since goodness is his responsibility, can it be not heavy? Since he stops discharging it only after death, can his way be not far?"

## 9

The Master said, "Poetry arouses a man; manners afford him ground to stand on; music completes him."

## 10

The Master said, "The masses may be led but cannot be made to comprehend."

## 11

The Master said, "Habitual recourse to bravado

and resentment against poverty end up in disturbance; inordinate contempt for others' failings, too, ends up in disturbance. "

## 12

The Master said, "Though talented and elegant like Prince Chou Kung, if a man is insolent and stingy, he is no more to be taken into account. "

## 13

The Master said, "A man who does not think of emolument when he has studied three years is seldom met with. "

## 14

The Master said, "Devout in belief and devoted to learning, one should not let go virtuous ways even for dear life.

"One need not enter a country showing disquieting signs, nor linger in one in chaos. When there is moral order in the world, one should be active but go into seclusion when moral disorder prevails.

"In a well-ruled country, poverty and obscurity

are to be regarded shameful, but, in a disordered one, wealth and position are."

## 15

The Master said, "Do not talk of policies when you are not in a position to make them."

## 16

The Master said, "It was not long after Chih was appointed Grand Master of Music that I heard a piece performed under his direction. Oh! How the tumultuous harmony of the last movement filled our fond ears to the overflowing!"

## 17

The Master said, "Nowadays people are extreme yet dishonest, ignorant yet forward, idiotic yet deceitful. I just do not know how to account for them."

## 18

The Master said, "Learn as frantically as you would run to catch up with one far ahead; hold tenaciously what you have learned lest you should lose it."

# 19

The Master said, "How lofty and unapproachable were Shun and Yü who, having all the world under their feet, remained disinterested!"

# 20

The Master said, "What a great ruler Yao was! So lofty and unapproachable was he. Heaven alone is great and Yao alone copied it. His merit was so immense and vast that the people did not know how to name it.

"Preeminent was his achievement and dazzling was his cultural enlightenment."

# 21

Shun had five assistants and the world was put in order.

King Wu said, "We have ten administrators."

The Master said, "'Capable men are scarce.' This certainly is a fact. Though, in the matter of talents, Chou was next only to the transition period from Yao's reign to Shun's, it had only nine men, one of the number being a woman.

"Though Chou had two-thirds of the world under

its rule, it willingly remained subject to Yin. It can indeed be said that Chou practised supreme virtues."

## 22

The Master said, "I just adore Yü. Economizing his own food, he made sumptuous offerings to deities; dressing himself plainly, he had resplendent knee covers and head-gear for occasions of offerings; having a cheap house for himself, he spent enormously on irrigation canals. I just adore Yü."

# CHAPTER IX
## The Master Seldom Spoke...

### 1

The Master seldom spoke about gain, providence and goodness.

### 2

A certain person from Ta Hsiang said, "Confucius is great but still, for all his erudition, he has no single achievement to his name."

Hearing this, the Master said to his disciples, "What shall I do, driving or shooting? I will rather choose driving."

### 3

The Master said, "A hemp hat is ritually required, but nowadays one made of pure silk is in vogue. As it is more economical, I will follow the majority.

"To bow below is the correct manner, but nowadays they bow when they get on to the floor. As it looks discourteous, I will bow below, though it is against the majority."

## 4

The Master made a point of repressing four propensities: wilfulness, predetermination, inflexibility, self-centeredness.

## 5

The Master was nearly mobbed in K'uang, taken for a popularly hated man.

He said, "Since King Won is gone, is culture not in my keeping? If it were Heaven's will to destroy this culture, I would not have been allowed to take part in it. Since manifestly it is not Heaven's will, what can the people of K'uang do to me?"

## 6

The Premier of Wu asked Tzu Kung, "Can the Master be a sage? Why has he so many skills then?"

Tzu Kung replied, "He is, no doubt, a predestined sage of great eminence. He has come, however, to possess many skills, too."

Hearing it, the Master said, "The Prime Minister knows me. As I was poor when young, I had to learn many lowly things. Has a man of virtue to master many trades? Certainly not. "

Lao remarked, "The Master used to say that he had had to learn trades for lack of proper government employment. "

## 7

The Master said, "What do I know? I know nothing. Sometimes cornered by a query from an ignoramus, I feel myself empty. Frantically scraping it together, I find my stock of knowledge exhausted, the question remaining still unanswered. "

## 8

The Master said, "The phoenix does not appear as it did in the times of the Emperor Shun and King Won, nor does the river throw up, as it did in the days of Sage Fu Hsi, a symbolic design about statecraft, I am through. "

## 9

Whenever a man in mourning or in court dress or a blind man appeared, the Master stood up in deference to them, though they were younger than himself. In passing them, he walked deferentially.

## 10

Yen Yüan said (on the personality of Confucius), sighing, "The more I look up, the higher it looks; the deeper I drill, the harder it feels. When I fancy it is in front, it is mysteriously at my back.

"The Master has a way of instructing people naturally and by stages. He broadened me with culture and girded me with manners.

"I can not break away from it and by the time my strength is exhausted, I feel myself confronted with what seems to stand towering. Desirous as I am to gain its top, I am helpless, no power left me."

## 11

The Master fell ill and Tzu Lu made one of the disciples his official steward— a thing not proper for a retired official like Confucius.

Between relapses, the Master said, "Yu (the personal name of Tzu Lu) has long been playing tricks on me! I am prohibited to have an official steward and yet I have one. Whom am I cheating? I am cheating Heaven.

"Moreover, I would rather die in the hands of

you my disciples than in those of an official steward. Even though I fail to get a grand funeral. shall I rot on the road?"

## 12

Tzu Kung asked, "Here is, say, a precious stone of the first water. Shall we put it away in a case or seek to sell it for a good price?"

The Master answered, "Sell it! Why, of course, sell it! I am waiting for a purchaser."

## 13

The Master expressed his wish to live among the nine uncivilized tribes. Someone said, "What about their vulgarity?"

The Master replied, "Where a gentleman lives, there cannot be any vulgarity."

## 14

The Master said, "Since I had come back to Lu from Wei, the musical compositions were rectified and the Poems were rearranged so as to fall into their proper places."

# 15

The Master said, "A man should serve his superiors abroad and his father and elder brother at home, pay special attention to funerals and take care not to get drunk. None of these now applies to me."

# 16

By the side of a stream, the Master said, "All things move on like this, never stopping day and night."

# 17

The Master said, "I am yet to see a person who is as fond of virtues as of women."

# 18

The Master said, "It is like making a hill. If I stop short of the last basketful of earth, it is I that do. It is like leveling ground. If I advance to throw just one single basketful of earth, it is I that do."

# 19

The Master said, "It is Hui that, when told a

thing, diligently pursues it to the finish. "

## 20

The Master said about Yen Yüan, "Alas! I only saw him advance and never saw him stop. "

## 21

The Master said, "There are those that sprout but fail to put out ears; there are those that put out ears but fail to bear grains. "

## 22

The Master said, "The younger generation is to be regarded with awe. Who dare say that they will be inferior to the people of today? But those who fail to be noticeable in their forties or fifties do not deserve to be regarded with awe, either. "

## 23

The Master said, "Who will not promise to comply with just and straight words of remonstration? What is to be valued is to repent. Who will not be pleased with courteous and roundabout expressions of exhortation? What is to be valued is to interpret them into points. I can do nothing for those who are pleased and yet fail to grasp points or who promise to comply and yet fail to repent."

## 24

The Master said, "The leader of a great army can be captured, but the will of an individual can not be captured with force."

## 25

The Master said, "It is only Yu who, clad in worn-out, old-cotton-padded clothes, can stand unabashed in the midst of people in costly fur dresses.

"A Poem says, 'Be free from envy and covetousness and whatever you do cannot be evil.'"

Tzu Lu always chanted this Poem thereafter.

The Master said, "How can this teaching be sufficient to lead one to goodness?"

## 26

The Master said, "It is only after the cold season

arrives that we know that the pines outgreen other trees."

## 27

The Master said, "The wise never get perplexed; the good never worry; the brave never fear."

## 28

The Master said, "In admitting that a person is serious about learning, we must not assume that he is seeking the Truth; in admitting that a man is seeking the Truth, we must not assume that he is firmly established in it; in admitting that a man is firmly established in the Truth, we must not assume that he has mastered the art of moderation in its application."

## 29

An old poem says, "Hawthorn blossoms now flutter and turn. It is not that I do not think of you, but the distance is too great."

The Master said, "The poet did not think of his friend enough, after all. The distance would have been nothing."

# CHAPTER X

## At Home...

### 1

At his country home, the Master, plain and meek, seemed unable to express himself intelligibly.

At the royal shrine or Court, his utterance was clear but careful.

### 2

When he talked with an official of his own rank at Court, his voice was clear and energetic. When talking with his official superior, his voice was genial but subdued.

When the Prince appeared in Court, he seemed uneasy from respect, while attentive.

### 3

When the Prince sent him word to receive a foreign guest, he looked taut and his toes were drawn in, it seemed.

In saluting, he joined his slightly raised hands

in front, standing so still that his dress fell straight,
front or back.

In stepping forward, he held his arms like the
poised wings of a bird.

When the guest was gone, he made a point of
reporting it to the Prince, saying, "The guest has
stopped looking back."

### 4

As he entered the Public Gate, he seemed to bow
as if it were too low.

He took care not to stand in the middle of the
gateway, nor to tread the threshold when walking.

In passing the standing-platform for the Prince in
the outer court, he changed color, his toes seemed
drawn in and he spoke falteringly.

While going up the steps to the audience room,
holding up the skirts, he looked as if he were bowing
and bated his breath as if he had stopped breathing
altogether.

Walking down the first step, his face recovered
color and became relaxed. Getting down all the steps,
he walked briskly, holding his arms like the poised
wings of a bird. Returning to his position, he again
looked uneasy from respect.

# 5

At a foreign court as envoy, he held the jade tablet (a symbol of authorization) stooping as if weighed down by it. He raised it in the posture of saluting and lowered it in that of presenting. He wore a tense, fearful look and took shortened steps, treading with the heel.

While he was presenting his own prince's gift to the host prince, color returned to his countenance.

When he presented his personal present to the host prince in a private audience, he was relaxed and genial.

# 6

He did not dye his collar cloth with any mixed color of red and blue, nor did he have his underwear made of red or purple cloth.

In summer, he wore thin hemp clothes, but always over underwear.

For various formal occasions, he had a black robe lined with black-sheepskin, a white robe lined with dearskin and a yellow robe lined with foxskin.

For home wear, he had a long fur robe made, only the righthand sleeve shortened for convenience.

He used a night gown one half again as long as himself.

At home, he wore clothes made of fox or sable skin as thick and comfortable.

The mourning period over, there was no ornament he refrained from wearing.

Clothes not for ceremonial occasions were cut to suit his convenience.

He never made a visit of condolence in black-sheepskin robe and black hat (reserved for happy occasions).

On the first day of each new month, he saluted toward the north in full court dress in remembrance of his old prince.

### 7

During purification, he kept lights burning and wore hemp clothes. He had a special diet, avoiding all greasy foods, and did not sit in the usual spot.

### 8

Rice could not be cleaned too much; taken raw, meat could not be chopped too finely.

He refused to eat rice out of taste or rotten fish or meat. He did not eat any food evil-colored or foul-smelling or not done to a turn or not in its own season.

He refused to take any food not properly cut or without the proper sauce.

He did not take too much meat in proportion to the rice. Though he did not set any limit to drinking, he did not drink so much as to get groggy.

He never drank purchased wine or ate dried meat bought from the street.

He took ginger every meal.

He never ate too much.

He saw that the meat offered to spirits was distributed before the night was over in the case of offerings of the royal household and within three days in the case of those of his own. Beyond the three days he prohibited eating it.

He did not answer questions with food in his mouth; he did not speak in bed.

Even though what he was eating was nothing but poor rice and vegetable soup, he always took a small portion of each food and piously deposited between the dishes in memory of his forebears.

## 9

He did not take a seat placed askant.

# 10

From drinking parties in his native place, he did not go away until an old man with a walking stick did.

While his rustic neighbors had a noisy session of exorcism—an immemorial superstition—he stood it out over the steps reserved for him in his old court dress.

# 11

When a messenger was sent to a friend in another country, he always made two deep bows to him in deference to his friend.

K'ang Tzu sent him some medicine, which he received after doing obeisance to the messenger, saying, "I don't know this medicine, so I cannot drink it."

# 12

Fire consumed his stable while he was away at Court. On coming home, he asked if any person had been harmed but did not inquire about the horses.

## 13

When the Prince sent him food, he righted his seat and tasted it first of all. If it was raw meat or fish, he boiled it and offered it first to his ancestors' spirits. If it was a live thing, he kept it.

When he dined with the Prince, he let him make the mealtime offering to his ancestors. He sampled each dish before the Prince started eating.

When the Prince visited him in illness, he laid his head to the east, his court dress spread over him with the belt thrown across it.

When the Prince sent for him, he started out walking, not waiting for the carriage to be readied.

## 14

When a friend of his, dying, had no relation to take care of his body, he readily said, "I will keep him shrouded and coffined until the burial."

He received a gift from a friend, be it a carriage with horses, without making obeisance, unless it was oblation meat.

## 15

He did not sleep in the posture suggestive of a corpse.

He did not put on a studied expression at home.

He did not let familiarity excuse him from changing color at meeting a person in mourning for his father or mother. He never met with an official or a blind man without making a polite gesture, no matter how intimate he might be with him.

Driving past a mourner or a person carrying records of census registration, he did not fail to lean over the cross-bar of the carriage as if bowing.

When a sumptuous feast was laid out for him, he changed color rising by way of expressing that he did not deserve it.

Whenever a thunder-storm or a strong gale started, he changed color.

## 16

As he got into a carriage, he took hold of the strap in an upright posture.

In the carriage, he did not turn his head round to observe objects in it, nor did he ejaculate or point with his finger.

## 17

At the slightest sign of alarm, the birds took wing, flew round and then settled on the ground again in a flock.

The Master said, "Look! How in season that female pheasant on the gorge bridge is!" Tzu Lu made a move to capture it. It clucked three times and then took wing.

# CHAPTER XI
## The First Period of Chou...

### 1

The Master said, "The manners and music of the first period of Chou are regarded crude like a rustic, while those of the latter period refined like an accomplished gentleman.

"If I ever come into my own, however, I will uphold the things of the first period."

### 2

The Master said, "None of those that followed me in Ch'en or Ts'ai are any longer with me.

"Yen Yüan, Min Tzu Ch'ien, Jan Po Niu and Chung Kung were outstanding in the practice of virtues, Ts'ai Wo and Tzu Kung in elocution, Jan Yu and Chi Lu in administration and Tzu Yu and Tzu Hsia in literature."

### 3

The Master said, "Hui is not so helpful to me, for he only exults at every word I utter."

## 4

The Master said, "Min Tzu Ch'ien is filial indeed! He allows no one to get between him and his parents or him and his brothers."

## 5

Nan Jung repeatedly read the Poems on temperance of words and Confucius married his elder brother's daughter to him.

## 6

When Chi K'ang Tzu asked which of his disciples was most devoted to learning, Confucius answered, "There was one Yen Hui very fond of learning but unfortunately he died young. There is none like him now."

## 7

When Yen Yüan died, his father Yen Lu asked Confucius for his carriage to pay for an outer coffin.

The Master said, "Every man is for his own son, gifted or ungifted. When my son Li died, I provided

him with only a simple coffin with no outer one.
I do not mean to walk in order to provide your son
with one. As a former ranking official, I do not
find walking becoming."

## 8

When Yen Yüan died, the Master lamented, "Woe
is me! Heaven has smitten me! Heaven has smitten
me!"

## 9

When Yen Yüan died, the Master cried his heart
out. His disciples reminded him of it.

The Master said, "Did I? If not for this man,
for whom shall I ever cry my heart out?"

## 10

When Yen Yüan died, the disciples wanted to
give him a big funeral. The Master said, "It is not
ritually correct." However, they did.

The Master said to them, "Hui regarded me as
his father. But I have failed to treat him as my
son. It is you, not me."

# 11

When Chi Lu asked how to serve spirits, the Master said, "Unable to serve men, how can you serve spirits?"

Again asked about death, he answered, "Not knowing life, how can you know death?"

# 12

While waiting upon Confucius, Min Tzu spoke in a genial but subdued voice, Tzu Lu in an impetuous and unrestrained manner, and Jan Yu and Tzu Kung in a clear and energetic way. The Master was serenely receptive to all.

The Master said, "Probably Yu(Tzu Lu)will not die a natural death."

# 13

The Kingdom of Lu was renovating its treasure house. Min Tzu Ch'ien said, "They might just as well leave it as it was. Why all this fuss of rebuilding?"

The Master said, "This man seldom opens his mouth, but, if he does, he has a point."

## 14

The Master said, "Why should Yu's (the personal name of Tzu Lu) harp be twanged at Ch'iu's (the personal name of Confucius) door?"

Thereafter, the disciples held themselves aloof from Tzu Lu. Noticing this, the Master said, "Yu has already entered the hall. He has only to enter the room."

## 15

When Tzu Kung inquired who was better, Ssu (Tzu Chang) or Shang (Tzu Hsia), the Master answered, "Ssu is over and Shang is short."

"Is Ssu better then?"

"Excess is just as bad as shortness."

## 16

Chi was richer than Prince Chou Kung had ever been and yet Jan Ch'iu extorted contributions from the people to make him richer.

The Master said, "He is not one of us. Denounce him, beating drums."

## 17

The Master said, "Ts'ai is half-witted; Ts'an is

dull; Ssu is showy; Yu is crude."

The Master said, "Hui is near the mark; he is often penniless.

"Tz'u does not accept his lot resignedly and makes money. However, his speculations often turn out true."

## 18

When Tzu Chang inquired about a man of natural goodness, the Master said, "He does not go by precepts, nor is he to enter the sanctum."

## 19

The Master said, "Is earnestness in discourse a mark of a virtuous man or of a pretender to virtue?"

## 20

When Tzu Lu inquired whether he should carry out what he heard at once, the Master replied, "How can you do so when your father and elder brother are with you?"

Asked the same question by Jan Yu, the Master said, "Of course, you should." Kung Hsi Hua expressed his bewilderment, asking why he had given two diametrically different answers to the selfsame question. The Master said, "As Ch'iu is timid, I wanted to encourage him; as Yu is foolhardy, I wanted to discourage him."

## 21

After a mob danger in K'uang, Yen Yüan showed himself last, when the Master said, "I had given you up-for dead." Yen Yüan replied, "How dared I die while you were living?"

## 22

Chi Tzu Jan asked whether Chung Yu and Jan Ch'iu deserved to be made ministers.

The Master said, "I thought you were raising a question about some extraordinary persons. Is it only about Yu and Ch'iu, after all?

"A worthy minister serves his prince with principles, which unaccepted, he should resign. Now Yu and Ch'iu are just nominal ministers."

"Do you mean then that they are only followers?"

"Well, they, too, will not follow in patricide or parricide."

## 23

When Tzu Lu appointed Tzu Kao, a man of fine character but with no learning, to the magistracy of Pi, the Master said, "You are spoiling an honest man."

Tzu Lu said, "Here are the people and here are the deities of Earth and Grain. Why should one need to do book-reading in order to gain practical knowledge?"

The Master said, "There! That is why I hate a man with an artful tongue."

## 24

Once when Tzu Lu, Tseng Hsi, Jan Yu and Kung Hsi Hua were with him, the Master said, "Is it on your mind that I am a bit older than you? Don't mind it at all this once.

"You always complain that no one knows you. Suppose someone does and uses you, what will you do?"

Tzu Lu readily answered, "If I am put in charge of a nation of one thousand chariots, sandwiched between two great powers, harassed by warfare and stricken by repeated famines, within three years, I

will make the people brave and responsible as well."
Thereupon, the Master smiled.

The Master asked Jan Ch'iu, "What is your say?"
He replied, "If I am entrusted with a country sixty
odd or fifty odd *li* square, within three years, I will
enable the people to enjoy ample livelihood. As for
teaching them manners and music, I shall have to
await an abler man."

The Master turned to Kung Hsi Hua, saying, "Ch'ih
(Kung Hsi Hua's personal name), what have you to
say?" He replied, "I cannot say that I can do anything. I only want to learn. When the Prince has
something to do about ancestral commemoration or
an assembly of princes, I want to be his petty assistant in ceremonial dress."

The Master then asked Tseng Hsi, "Tien (Tseng
Hsi's personal name), what will you do?" He had
been strumming a harp in a leisurely manner. Putting down his instrument with a slight bang, he
stood up respectfully and answered, "Mine is very
different from the choices of my three friends." The
Master encouraged him, saying, "Well, what harm
to speak out? It is only each speaking his own
mind." Thereupon Tseng Hsi said, "In late spring,
I would rather go out in a new spring dress with
several companions and half-dozen lads and, after
bathing in the River Ki and sauntering around the

scenic Wu Yü, come home singing. " Here the Master said, sighing, "I am with you, Tien. "

Lingering after the other three went away, Tseng Hsi asked, "How were the answers of my three friends?" The Master answered, "They only expressed their own wishes. That is all. "

"Master, why did you smile at Yu's answer?"

"A nation is to be ruled with courtesy. His words did not sound so modest, so I smiled. "

"Did what Ch'iu said not also concern a realm?"

"Why, of course. A tract of land sixty odd or fifty odd *li* square cannot be anything else. "

"Didn't Ch'ih's words, too, concern a realm?"

"Of course, yes. What did he say except princely matters? Though he belittled the function of assisting a prince, who could expect to do a greater thing?"

# CHAPTER XII
## Yen Yüan...

### 1

When Yen Yüan inquired what goodness was, the Master said, "To control oneself into proper manners is to attain goodness. If a man controls himself into proper manners one single day, the world will be inclined toward goodness thereby. One attains goodness as one exerts for it. How can one rely on others for it?"

Requested by Yen Yüan to give concrete terms, the Master said, "Do not see an improper thing; do not hear an improper thing; do not say an improper thing; do not do an improper thing."

Yen Yüan said, "For all my dullness, let me mind this teaching forever."

### 2

When Chung Kung inquired about goodness, the Master said, "Act abroad as if you were receiving a great guest; use the people as if you were officiating in a great sacrifice. Above all, do not impose on others what you do not like yourself. Then you will not be complained against either in the nation or in the family."

Chung Kung said, "Though unworthy, I will mind this teaching forever."

## 3

When Ssu Ma Niu inquired about goodness, the Master said, "A good man does not speak with ease."

"If a man does not speak easily, then can he be called good?"

"As it is difficult to carry out what a man says, can he say anything with ease?"

## 4

When Ssu Ma Niu asked about a man of virtue, the Master said, "A man of virtue never worries, nor fears."

Again asked whether a man could be called virtuous, if he neither worried nor feared, the Master answered, "As self-searching brings out no remorse, what ground is there for worry or fear?"

## 5

Ssu Ma Niu said sadly, "People all have brothers, but I have none."

Thereupon Tzu Hsia said, "I hear that life and

death are fixed by destiny and that wealth and poverty are dispensed by providence.

"If a gentleman is respectful without slackening and, in dealing with people, humble and courteous, everyone in the world can be his brother. Why should he worry because he has no brothers?"

# 6

When Tzu Chang inquired about clear-mindedness, the Master replied, "If a man is swayed by no insidious slander or personal wound in his judgment of people, he can be called clear-minded. He can even be called far-sighted."

# 7

Asked by Tzu Kung on statecraft, the Master said, "It consists of ample livelihood, adequate defense and popular confidence."

Tzu Kung asked, "If you have to drop one of the three, which will you drop first?"

"Defense."

"If you again have to drop one of the two, which will you do?"

"Livelihood. All have died since immemorial times, but a state cannot stand without popular confidence."

## 8

Chi Tzu Ch'eng said, "A man of virtue should solely mind character-building. Why should he devote himself to culture?"

Tzu Kung said, "How regrettable is his remark about a man of virtue! A slip of the tongue is not to be overtaken by the fleetest horses and retrieved. Character and culture are correlated and concomitant. Removing culture is like burning the hair off a tiger's or a leopard's skin. Their hide looks just like a dog's or a sheep's."

## 9

Prince Ai Kung asked Yu Jo, "Famine has caused deficits and what is the remedy?"

Yu Jo answered, "Why do you not go back to the tax system of Chou, taking one-tenth of what the people produce?"

"Taking two-tenths, I still have deficiency. How can I take less?"

"If the people have enough, how can you alone have deficiency? If they have deficiency, how can you alone have enough?"

# 10

When Tzu Chang asked how to strengthen virtue and discern inconsistency, the Master said, "Emphasis on sincerity and faithfulness and compliance with whatever is just and right strengthen virtue.

"A man wishes another to live, if he loves him, and wishes him to die, if he hates him. If a man wishes another to live and then again wishes him to die, that is inconsistency."

# 11

Prince Ching Kung of Ch'i asked Confucius for his opinion on statecraft. The Master replied, "Statecraft is nothing but prince behaving like prince, subject like subject, father like father and son like son."

The Prince said, "You have said well. Should they fail to behave as they ought to respectively, could I even eat, no matter how much grain I had?"

# 12

The Master said, "It is only Yu that can adjudicate a case of litigation with one word."

Tzu Lu would leave no promise unfulfilled.

## 13

The Master said, "In hearing a litigation case, I should be no better than others. But my aim is rather to enable the people to dispense with litigation altogether."

## 14

When Tzu Chang inquired about statecraft, the Master said, "Be not idle and lax when alone, and deal with people with loyalty."

## 15

The Master said, "A great man will assist others to come to good and never aid them to go to evil. But a small man acts to the contrary."

## 16

When Chi K'ang Tzu inquired about statecraft, the Master said, "The essence of statecraft is justice. If you lead with justice, who can dare to be unjust?"

## 17

When Chi K'ang Tzu, worrying about stealing,

asked Confucius the way of stopping it, he replied,
"If you cease to be covetous yourself, the people
will not steal, even if encouraged."

## 18

Chi K'ang Tzu asked Confucius, "What do you
think of it, if I help the people grow moral by
killing off the crooked and immoral?"

Confucius answered, "Why must you kill in order
to rule a country? If you wish to be kind, the people will be kind, too. A great man is like wind,
while petty people are like grass. The grass will
lie while the wind passes over it."

## 19

Tzu Chang asked, "What must a man of learning
do to be successful?"

The Master retorted, "What do you mean by successful?"

Tzu Chang replied, "I mean notable in one's
family and country."

"That is notable, not successful. A man who will
succeed is plain and straight, loves justice, hears
discriminatingly what people say, studying their
expressions, and is considerate and humble in dealing

with people. Such a man will always succeed in the nation and in the family.

"A man that will be notable has the astuteness to appear charitable while acting contrarily and keeps at it unperturbed. Such a man is sure to be noted in the nation and in the family."

## 20

While recreating at the foot of Mt. Wu Yü, Fan Ts'u asked Confucius the way to strengthen virtue, uproot hidden evils and discern inconsistency.

The Master said, "That is a very good question. If you work first and think of gain afterwards, virtue will be strengthened; if you fight your own evil without attacking the evil in others, it will tend to remove hidden evils; if you forget yourself in momentary anger for your parents' sake and bring calamity on them, is this not inconsistency?"

## 21

When Fan Ts'u inquired about goodness, the Master said, "It is loving people." Again inquired about intelligence, he said, "It is knowing people."

As Fan Ts'u did not comprehend it, the Master explained, saying, "Raising the straight and leaving the crooked will make the crooked straight."

Fan Ts'u later met Tzu Hsia and asked, "The other day, when I asked the Master what intelligence was, he answered, 'Raising the straight and leaving the crooked will make the crooked straight.' What does that mean?"

Tzu Hsia replied, "What a profound remark that is. When Shun had the empire to rule, he elevated Kao Yao out of the multitude and the crooked could not get near him. When T'ang reigned over the empire, he elevated Yi Yin out of the multitude and the crooked could not get near him."

## 22

When asked by Tzu Kung about the art of association, the Master said, "Faithfully admonish your friend so as to keep him on the virtuous path, but, rebuffed, stop giving further advice so that you may not be disgraced."

## 23

Tseng Tzu said, "Gentlemen come together through cultural contacts and, in turn, round out their moral character through mutual association."

# CHAPTER XIII
## Tzu Lu...

### 1

When Tzu Lu asked about statecraft, the Master said, "The administrator must set an example himself and work hard."

Asked for more, he said, "Do that unflaggingly."

### 2

When Chung Kung who had become Chi's chief administrator asked about statecraft, the Master said, "You must practise everything yourself in advance of the officials under you, forgive their small mistakes and elevate the able."

"How can I know all the able men and use them?"

"If you use the able men you know, will others leave those they know?"

### 3

Tzu Lu asked, "If the Prince of Wei let you decide policies, what will you do first?"

The Master answered, "I would rectify human relationships first of all." Tzu Lu retorted, "I thought so! How unpractical! How will you rectify them?"

The Master said, "How can you be so crude? A gentleman never ventures an opinion on what he does not know. Human relationships not rectified, speech would grate; speech grating, activities would not carry on; activities not carrying on, manners and music would not flourish; manners and music not flourishing, punishments would not be administered with justice; punishments not justly administered, the people just would not know what to do.

"In rectifying human relationships, a man of virtue must have words to say. In saying words, he must have their practice in mind. The rule is that he should feel no scruple in speaking them."

## 4

When Fan Ts'u asked to be taught how to farm, the Master replied, "I am not so good as an old farm hand."

Again asked to teach gardening, the Master said, "I am not so good as an old gardener."

When Fan Ts'u was gone, the Master said, "What a petty soul Fan Hsü is! If an administrator is courteous, the people cannot but be respectful; if he is just, they cannot but obey; if he is faithful, they cannot but be loyal. Then people will come to him from all directions with their babies on their back. Why should he need farming himself?"

**5**

The Master said, "If a man, for all the three hundred Poems he has memorized, fails to make an efficient administrator, when given the chance, or to answer a question with authority, when sent abroad as envoy, what has the profusion benefited him?"

**6**

The Master said, "If a great man carries himself with rectitude, he will prevail without orders, but, if he fails to do so, the people will not follow him, even if expressly commanded. "

**7**

The Master said, "The institutions of Lu and Wei are much similar like brothers. "

## 8

The Master said, "Kung Tzu Ching of Wei knows the art of home-keeping. When he first had a home bare and empty, he said, 'It is about agreeable.' When he had immediate necessaries, he said, 'It is about complete.' When he had plenty, he said, 'It is about perfect.'"

## 9

As the Master was going to Wei, Jan Yu drove his carriage. He said, looking round the country, "It is pretty populous." Thereupon, Jan Yu asked, "If so, what is to be added?"

"To make them rich."

"When they have been made rich, what is to be added?"

"To instruct them."

## 10

The Master said, "Should someone use me, order would begin to prevail in a year and be fully established in three years."

## 11

The Master said, "There is an old adage saying,

'A century of benevolent rule may succeed in win-
ning over the criminal elements of the community
and dispensing with the capital punishment at last.'
This is a very truthful saying. "

## 12

The Master said, "Even for a sage–ruler, a generation
is necessary to win the entire people to goodness. "

## 13

The Master said, "If a man can carry himself with
rectitude, can administration be a problem to him?
But, if he can not, how can he ever hope to rectify
others?"

## 14

Seeing Jan Tzu coming from Court, the Master
asked him, "Why are you late?" Jan Tzu answered,
"Some state affairs held me. " Thereupon, the Master
said, "You mean his private affairs? If they had been
state affairs, I should have known them, though I
no longer hold an office in the Government. "

# 15

When Prince Ting Kung asked, "Is there one sentence that can make a state prosper, when lived up to?"

The Master replied, "A sentence cannot exactly do that but one may almost. They say that to be a king is hard and to be a subject is not easy, too. If a king is aware that it is hard to be a king, will it not almost make a state prosper?"

Prince Ting Kung again asked, "Is there one sentence that can ruin a state?" The Master answered, "No sentence can exactly do that but one may almost. I hear it said, 'I have no pleasure to be king except that whatever I may say is obeyed.' If what he says is good, it is well that it is obeyed, but, suppose what he says is evil and yet is obeyed, will it not almost ruin a state?"

# 16

When Prince Yieh Kung inquired about statecraft, the Master replied, "Let those near you be pleased and those far-away will be drawn to you."

# 17

On becoming the magistrate of Chü Fu, Tzu Hsia

inquired about statecraft. The Master replied, "Do not hurry; do not seek petty profits. Hurrying, one cannot succeed. Seeking small profits, one cannot carry through a great cause."

## 18

Prince Yieh Kung said to Confucius, "I know of a man in our community, who is bolt upright. His father stole a sheep and he bore witness to it."

In reply, the Master said, "The upright in our community are different from that. The son hides the father's faults and the father the son's. Still there is uprightness."

## 19

When Fan Ts'u inquired about goodness, the Master said, "Be pious when alone; handle affairs reverently; be sincere with people. Do not let go these practices, even if you be among a barbarian tribe."

## 20

Tzu Kung asked, "How should one behave to be called a man of culture?" The Master replied, "If he carries himself with honor and, as envoy, does not disgrace the message of his prince, he may be called a man of culture. "

"Who is next?"

"A man who is regarded filial by his own family circles and respectful by the countryside. "

"Who is again next?"

"The one who invariably keeps his given word and carries out without fail what he has once set his hands on may be the next man, though of a petty, stereotyped sort. "

"What do you think of the current statesmen?"

"They are all men of small caliber, not worthy to be counted. "

# 21

The Master said, "If I fail to find men of golden mean to associate with, I would rather choose the extreme or narrow-minded. The extreme sometimes venture for better things, while the narrow-minded refrain from certain vices. "

# 22

The Master said, "A southern proverb says, 'Without steadiness, one cannot even make a witch or doctor.' How true this saying is! The Book of

Changes says, 'If one does not constantly keep to virtuous ways, one will come to disgrace.'"

The Master said, "It is best, however, not to betake oneself to fortune-telling at all, even on the basis of the Book of Changes."

## 23

The Master said, "A great man is conciliatory but not conformable, while a small man is conformable but not conciliatory."

## 24

Tzu Kung asked, "How is it to be liked by everybody in the countryside?" The Master replied, "Not good." Again asked how it was to be hated by the entire countryside, the Master said, "Not good, either. It is better to be liked by the good and hated by the bad of them."

## 25

The Master said, "A great man is easy to serve but hard to please. He is not pleased, if one tries to please him in a questionable way. But he uses a man for a definite function. On the other hand, a small man is hard to serve but easy to please, for

he is pleased, even though one tries to please him
by an improper means, while expecting his man to
be perfect in every way. "

## 26

The Master said, "A great man is weighty but not
haughty, while a small man is haughty but not
weighty. "

## 27

The Master said, "Hardness, stubbornness, stolidity
and dumbness are allied to goodness. "

## 28

When Tzu Lu asked what manner of man might
be called a man of culture, the Master said, "One
who is considerate, circumspect and genial can be called
a man of culture—considerate and circumspect with
one's friends and genial with one's brothers. "

## 29

The Master said, "Instructed seven years by a benevolent leader, a people may be ready for their

country's defense."

# 30

The Master said, "To throw the uninstructed masses into battle is called an act of abandoning the people."

# CHAPTER XIV
## Hsien Inquired...

### 1

When Hsien inquired what shame was, the Master said, "It is honorable to get government salary when the nation is well ruled, but it is shameful when it is misruled."

### 2

Again asked whether refraining from contention, display, resentment and covetousness could constitute goodness, the Master replied, "It makes a difficult thing, no doubt, but I do not know whether it constitutes goodness."

### 3

The Master said, "A man of culture who feels attached to a position is not worthy of the name."

### 4

The Master said, "When the country is well ruled,

one should speak fearlessly and act fearlessly but, when it is misruled, one should act fearlessly but speak modestly."

## 5

The Master said, "A virtuous man is bound to speak good words but one who says good words does not necessarily possess virtue; a good man is bound to be courageous but one who is courageous is not necessarily good."

## 6

Nan Kung Kua said to Confucius, "Yi of the Hsia Dynasty was a skilled archer and Ao could tow a ship but both did not die a natural death. Yü and Chi, on the other hand, ruled the empire while engaged in farming." The Master made no response. When Nan Kung Kua went away, he said, "That is a virtuous man. How he thirsts after virtue!"

## 7

The Master said, "There may be some men of caliber who are not good, but no small man can ever be good."

**8**

The Master said, "How can a man help toiling for the one he loves or rectifying, through persuasion, the one, to whom he is loyal?"

**9**

The Master said, "In preparing a state message to a neighboring prince, Pi Ch'en makes the rough draft, Shih Shu analyses it, Grand Receptionist Tzu Yü revises it and Tzu Ch'an gives it the finishing touches."

**10**

Asked by someone about Tzu Ch'an, the Master said, "He is a charitable man."

Asked about Kuan Hsi, he said, "Ah, that fellow!"

Asked about Kuan Chung, he said, "He took Pien Yi, a town of three hundred houses, from Po, who, though reduced thereby to indigence, to the end of his life, never said a complaining word against him."

**11**

The Master said, "It is difficult to live in poverty

without bitterness; it is easy to live in affluence
without arrogance."

## 12

The Master said, "Though Meng Kung Ch'iao is
more than qualified to be a grand steward of a big
country like Chao or Wei, he cannot make a state
minister of even a small nation like T'eng or Hsüeh."

## 13

When Tzu Lu asked about a fully rounded man, the
Master answered, "If a man combines in himself
Chang Wu Chung's intelligence, Meng Kung Ch'iao's
incorruptibility, Pien Chuang Tzu's courage and Jan
Ch'iu's tact, topping them all with the elegance of
manners and music, he may well be called a fully
rounded person.

"What goes by the name nowadays, however, need
not be all that. A man who thinks of justice in
the face of gain, who risks his life for a friend in
danger and who does not forget an old promise may
also pass for one."

## 14

Confucius asked Kung Ming Chia about Kung Shu

Won Tzu, "Is it true that your master never speaks, never smiles and never takes?"

Kung Ming Chia replied, "Your informer went too far. My master speaks only at an appropriate moment and nobody is tired of hearing him. He smiles only when really pleased and nobody feels bored with it. He takes only when it is just to take and nobody grumbles about it." Thereupon, the Master wondered aloud, " Is it true? Can it be?"

## 15

The Master said, "Tsang Wu Chung, after repairing to Fang and entrenching himself there, sent in a recommendation on the succession question. Though he says he did not threaten our Prince, I do not believe it."

## 16

The Master said, "Prince Won Kung of Chin was wily and not upright, while Prince Huan Kung of Ch'i was upright and not wily."

## 17

Tzu Lu said, "When Prince Huan Kung of Ch'i

murdered his younger brother Chiu, Shao Hu, a follower, died with him, while Kuan Chung, also his follower, did not die. What do you think of Kuan Chung? He was not good enough, was he?"

The Master answered, "Huan Kung effected a working federation of all the princes peacefully, not through force of arms. It was entirely due to Kuan Chung. He was that good."

## 18

Tzu Kung said, "Kuan Chung can not have been a good man. When Prince Huan Kung killed his younger brother Chiu, he not only failed to follow him in death but later went over to the murderer's side."

The Master responded, "Kuan Chung aided Prince Huan Kung to align the princes and stay the crumbling empire against the marauding barbarians. We are still indebted to the event. But for him, I might dress myself in a barbarian style, with loose hair and the collar reversely overlapping. How could he have acted like a narrow-minded individual that strangles himself in the ditch, forsaken and forgotten?"

## 19

Kung Shu Won Tzu recommended his own steward

Chuan to his prince's favor so that he, in time, became a state minister in the same rank as his master. Hearing this, the Master said, "He is indeed worthy of the epithet 'won' (meaning culture)."

## 20

The Master once mentioned the immoral acts of Prince Ling Kung of Wei. K'ang Tzu asked, "Why, then, does this dissolute prince not get deposed?"

Confucius answered, "Chung Shu Yü has been put in charge of foreign envoys, Master of Rituals T'o in charge of the royal shrine, Wang Sun Chia in charge of the army. Putting proper persons in proper places like that, why should he fall?"

## 21

The Master said, "To profess immodestly promises little deed."

## 22

Ch'en Ch'eng Tzu murdered his prince Chien Kung.

Hearing this, Confucius, bathing himself by way of purification, repaired to Court and besought Prince Ai Kung to send a punitive expedition against the parricide. Thereupon, the Prince asked Confucius to consult the three houses.

Coming out, the Master said, "As one of the state ministers, I was duty-bound to make a recommendation to the Prince on the incident. Now the Prince tells me to consult the three houses!"

Confucius visited the three powerful houses, but all spoke against the expedition. "Well," said the Master, "as one of the state ministers, I was duty-bound to make a recommendation."

## 23

When Tzu Lu inquired about the way of serving a prince the Master answered, "Do not cheat and be aggressively direct."

## 24

The Master said, "A great man develops upward, while a small man develops downward."

## 25

The Master said, "Formerly, scholars studied to improve themselves, but nowadays they study for others to see."

## 26

Ch'ü Po Yü sent a messenger to Confucius, who, bidding him to sit, asked him what his master had been doing. The messenger answered, "My master has been exerting to reduce his failings and is not yet satisfied with the result." When he was gone, the Master exclaimed, "Excellent messenger! Excellent messenger!"

## 27

Tseng Tzu used to say, quoting from the Book of Changes, "The thoughts of a virtuous man never wander from his present duties."

## 28

The Master said, "A virtuous man tends to underdo in speech and overdo in deed."

## 29

The Master said, "A virtuous man has three mottoes, none of which I can justly claim for myself. The good never worry; the wise never puzzle; the courageous never fear."

Tzu Kung said, commenting, "This is what the master spoke about himself, though."

## 30

Tzu Kung criticized people. The Master said, "He must be very wise to do that. As for me, I just have not that much leisure."

## 31

The Master said, "Do not worry about men not knowing you. Rather worry about your having no ability to show."

## 32

The Master said, "He may be called a wise man, who does not look for deceit, nor anticipates treachery, and yet becomes aware of them just in time."

## 33

Wei Sheng Mou said to Confucius, "Why do you hang on wherever you go? Is it not for insinuating yourself into favor or influence?"

The Master answered, "I dare not aspire after that. I only want to avoid pig-headedness."

## 34

The Master said, "A good horse is praised not for its strength but for its breeding."

## 35

Someone asked, "What do you think of returning good for evil?"

The Master replied, "Then what will you return for good? Return justice for evil and return good for good."

## 36

The Master said, "No one knows me." Tzu Kung asked, "What do you mean by that?" The Master answered, "I do not grumble against Providence, nor find fault with men; I only endeavor to learn from low to high. Only Heaven knows me."

## 37

Kung Po Liao slandered Tzu Lu to Chi Sun and

Tzu Fu Ching Po, a colleague of Tzu Lu, reported it to Confucius, saying, "My master may be influenced by Kung Po Liao, but I still have power enough to kill him and display his corpse at Court." The Master said, "Is the Way to prevail? It will be providence. Is it to fail? It will be providence again. What can Kung Po Liao do to providence?"

## 38

The Master said, "The wise avoid the world itself; the next avoid the position; again the next avoid expression; still again the next avoid speech."

## 39

The Master said, "Seven men have already gone into seclusion."

## 40

While Tzu Lu put up at Shih Men (Stone Gate) for the night, the gatekeeper asked him where he had come from. Tzu Lu answered, "From Confucius." He said, "Isn't that the person who insists on doing what he knows he can't?"

## 41

In Wei, Confucius was once playing stone gongs, when a man carrying a basket on his back remarked as he passed by the house where Confucius was lodging, "How feelingly he plays the stone gongs!" By and by, he added, "How worldly the stubbornness! No one recognizing his ability, the best thing for him is to quit. 'In deep water, just wade but in a shallow wade, lifting the skirts.'"

The Master said. "Given up, there is no problem, of course!"

## 42

Tzu Chang asked, "The Book of History says, 'King Kao Tsung did not speak during the three-year mourning period.' What does it mean?"

The Master answered, "King Kao Tsung need not be singled out. The ancients all acted like him. When a prince died, all the officials stopped dealing with his successor and took orders from the premier instead for the ensuing three years."

## 43

The Master said, "If the ruler is strict in observing manners, the people will become docile."

new (...) The Master answered, "(...) all in
the (...) feels and walk (...) side by side.
It is not so much inconvenient as irwving of

## 44

When Tzu Lu inquired the way of becoming a
great man, the Master answered, "Build up your
character in a pious frame of mind."

"Is that all?"

"Build up your character so as to inspire your
friends with assurance."

"Is that enough?"

"Build up your character so as to inspire the people
with assurance. Even Yao and Shun regarded themselves short on this score."

## 45

Yüan Jang was waiting crouching when Confucius
appeared. The Master said, "When young, you were
unruly; grown up, you loafed your heyday away.
You are now decrepit and yet refuse to die. This
is how to be a social bane!" So saying, Confucius
tapped the old man's shin with his staff.

## 46

The Master made an errand boy of a lad from

the village of Ch'üeh. Someone asked, "Is he improving?" The Master answered, "I saw him sit in his elders' seats and walk with them side by side. It is not so much improvement as growing up quickly that he seems to be after."

# CHAPTER XV

## Prince Ling Kung of Wei...

### 1

When Prince Ling Kung of Wei asked Confucius about army formations, he answered, "I am informed on sacrificial rituals but not on army affairs." Confucius left Wei the next day.

Going without food in Ch'en, some of his followers lay prostrate. Tzu Lu said angrily to Confucius, "Is even a great man reduced to penury?" The Master answered, "Only a great man behaves in penury. A small man loses all self-control in it."

### 2

The Master said, "Tz'u (Tzu Kung's personal name), do you think that I am intelligent as a result of much learning?" Tzu Kung replied, "Yes. Is it not the case then?" The Master said, "No. It is the one single principle, with which I test all things."

The Master said, "Few attain virtue through intelligence."

145

## 3

The Master said, "It is Shun only that ruled the world, doing nothing himself. What did he do except sitting erect toward the south in humility?"

## 4

Tzu Chang asked about getting on.   The Master said, "If a man is sincere and reliable in speech and considerate and respectful in conduct, he would get acceptance even in a barbarian community. If he is, on the other hand, insincere and unreliable in speech and inconsiderate and disrespectful in conduct, would he be accepted even by his county folk?

"Getting up, we see it (probably the master principle of life impelling these behaviors) precede us; driving, we see it leaning against the cross-bar. Only thus we shall get acceptance."

Tzu Chang wrote it all down on his belt.

## 5

The Master said, "Remonstrant Yü was indeed arrow-straight.  He was like an  arrow when  the nation was ruled well. He was like an arrow even when it was misruled.

"How virtuous Ch'ü Po Yü was! He served in the government when the nation was well ruled but went into seclusion when it was misruled."

## 6

The Master said, "If you fail to speak with a man worthy to speak with, you will lose a man; if you speak with a man not worthy to speak with, you will lose your word. The wise do not lose a man, nor do they lose their word."

## 7

The Master said, "A dedicated man or a good man never mars his cause or virtue even to save his life but would rather lay it down in order to consummate his cause or virtue."

## 8

When Tzu Kung asked him about the way of doing good, the Master replied, "An artisan intent upon doing good jobs must first sharpen his tools. In like manner, in a country, one should choose the

ablest state minister to serve from among the many
and the best scholars to associate with out of the
numerous. "

## 9

When Yen Yüan inquired how to rule a nation,
the Master said, "Adopt the calendar of the Hsia
Dynasty; use the carriage of Yin; wear the hat of
Chou; confine music to that of the Emperor Shun;
banish the songs of Cheng, for they are licentious;
keep the honey-tongued men away, for they are
dangerous. "

## 10

The Master said, "A man without early precau-
tions must face immediate worries. "

## 11

The Master said, "It is all up: I have never seen
anyone love virtue as he loves a woman. "

## 12

The Master said, "Tsang Won Chung had, in a

sense, stolen his position, for he did not invite Liu
Hsia Hui to work with him in the government,
though he knew that he was abler than himself."

## 13

The Master said, "If a man blames himself more
and others less, he will avoid resentment."

## 14

The Master said, "For a man who does not say to
himself, 'What shall I do? What shall I do?' I can
do nothing indeed."

## 15

The Master said, "A man who never utters a just
word in company a whole day, only fond of resort-
ing to small tricks, will hardly come to any good."

## 16

The Master said, "A man of virtue regards justice
as essence. If a man practises it with manners, man-
ifests it with humility and carries it through with
fidelity, he is indeed a virtuous man."

## 17

The Master said, "A man of virtue is troubled by his own inability, not by the fact that people do not know him."

## 18

The Master said, "A man of virtue hates the idea of leaving nothing to remember him by after he is gone."

## 19

The Master said, "A great soul seeks everything within himself, while a petty man seeks everything from others."

## 20

The Master said, "A great man is full of self-respect but not contentious, gregarious but not partisan."

## 21

The Master said, "A great man does not use a man

because of his words, nor does he reject words because of the man that spoke them."

## 22

Tzu Kung asked, "Is there one word which can be our lifelong motto?" The Master replied, "Commiseration. Do not do to others what you do not wish to have done to yourself."

## 23

The Master said, "I have no prejudice to praise some and disparage others. If I happen to praise a certain man, it is because he has been tested.

"These are the same people as were treated with straightforwardness during the Three Golden Dynasties."

## 24

The Master said, "In my young days, I still met with historians leaving blanks to be filled later by greater scholars or people lending their horses to others. Now I see no more of them."

## 25

The Master said, "Sophistry vitiates virtue; petty

impatience overturns a big plan. "

## 26

The Master said, "Be circumspect instead of being credulous when someone is either hated by all or liked by all. "

## 27

The Master said, "It is man that expands religion, not religion that expands man. "

## 28

The Master said, "Not to repent when wrong is truly wrong. "

## 29

The Master said, "I once meditated day and night, taking neither food nor sleep. It proved availless. Nothing is like learning. "

## 30

The Master said, "A great man is concerned with

the right way of living, not with livelihood. Hunger is involved in farming, while salary is involved in learning. A great man cares about how to live, not what to eat. "

## 31

The Master said, "Whatever (a moral truth) is comprehended through intelligence will be lost again, unless it is secured with goodness.

"Whatever is comprehended through intellect and secured with goodness will not command popular respect, unless it is held with dignity.

"Whatever is comprehended through intellect, secured with goodness and held with dignity will not be effective, unless it is applied with manners. "

## 32

The Master said, "A great man should not know little and yet assume great responsibilities. On the other hand, a small man should not assume great responsibilities and can afford to know little. "

## 33

The Master said, "The people need goodness more

than fire or water. I have seen people burned or drowned to death, but I have never seen them die of goodness. "

## 34

The Master said, "In goodness, we need not yield precedence even to our teachers. "

## 35

The Master said, "A man of virtue is constant but not hidebound. "

## 36

The Master said, "In serving a prince, one should put service before remuneration. "

## 37

The Master said, "Instruction recognizes no class distinction. "

## 38

The Master said, "Men of different faiths need

not advise each other. "

## 39

The Master said, "The sole function of speech is to communicate ideas clearly. "

## 40

As Master of Music Mien (all music masters were blind) reached the steps, in a visit, the Master said to him, "Here are the steps. " As he reached a seat, he was likewise told that it was a seat. When all were seated, the Master told him who were present, saying, "So and so is sitting in such and such a place. "

When the master of music was gone, Tzu Chang asked, "Is that the way of conversing with music masters?" The Master answered, "Yes. That is the way of aiding them. "

# CHAPTER XVI
## Chi...

### 1

Chi was going to attack Chuan Yü. Jan Yu and Chi Lu came and told Confucius that Chi was preparing an incident against Chuan Yü.

Confucius said, "Ch'iu (Jan Yu's personal name), is it not your own blame? Chuan Yü is what long, long ago the then ruling King created as the chiefdom of Tung Meng and is situated in the middle of the kingdom. Its people are loyal subjects of the King. How could they be attacked?"

Jan Yu said, "Our master is after it. We two aren't."

Confucius said, "Ch'iu, don't you remember what Chou Jem said? 'Let all get into the rank with good plans but those who fail must retire.' Of what help are they who fail to support their master when he totters or to pull him up when fallen? Furthermore, your words exceeded propriety. If tigers and single-horned wild bulls get out of their cages or if a turtle or a precious stone is found damaged in its case, who is to blame? Not their keeper?"

Jan Yu said, "Chuan Yü is impregnable and close

to Pi. If it is not taken now, it will be a source
of trouble to our posterity. "

Confucius said, "Ch'iu, a man of virtue hates those
that, when they have a dirty motive, do not fail
to gloss over it with words. I have heard that a
ruler's or a family head's problem is not so much
dearth as uneven distribution, not so much poverty
as unrest, for poverty is not felt in evenness of
distribution, scantiness is not felt in harmony and
peace obviates subversion. Thus, when far-away peoples remain unsubmissive, they are treated with
civility and generosity until they submit. When they
do, they are helped to enjoy peace. But now, this is
how you Yu and Ch'iu assist your master: When a
far-away people is not submissive, you are unable
to induce it to submit; when the nation goes asunder,
you are unable to keep it together. Further, you are
scheming for a conflict within the nation. I fear that
Chi's source of trouble is not in Chuan Yü but in
his own household. "

## 2

The Master said, "When the world is well ruled,
orders on such matters as manners, music and warfare
are issued by the Emperor, but, when the world is
misruled, they are issued by princes. Then the empire

will hardly hold out for ten more generations. If they are issued by state ministers, the state can hardly hold out for five more generations. If the personal secretaries of a prince manipulate state affairs, the state can hardly hold out for three more generations.

"When the world is well ordered, policies will not be decided by state ministers, nor will politics be discussed by the masses."

### 3

The Master said, "The revenue has been five generations off the direct control of the Prince; the administrative power has been four generations in the hands of state ministers. Consequently, the descendants of Prince Huan Kung of Ch'i are obscure."

### 4

The Master said, "There are three kinds of helpful friends, and three kinds of harmful ones. Honest friends, scrupulous friends and widely informed friends are helpful. Foppish friends, flattering friends and sweet-tongued friends are harmful."

## 5

The Master said, "There are three kinds of beneficial pleasures and three kinds of harmful ones. Love of moderating manners and music, love of speaking of others' good acts and love of making many good friends are beneficial. Love of extravagance, love of loafing and love of feasting are harmful."

## 6

The Master said, "In waiting upon a great man, one is apt to reveal three shortcomings: to speak before it is time, which is called rashness; not to speak when it is time, which is called reservedness; to speak when he is in no mood to listen, which is called blindness."

## 7

The Master said, "There are three things, against which a man of virtue must be on guard: In youth, as his vigor still lacks stamina, he should guard against sexuality; in full manhood, as his vigor is at its height, he should guard against quarrels; in old age, as his vigor has declined, he should guard against gain."

## 8

The Master said, "A man of virtue holds three things in awe, providence, a great man and the teachings of a sage.

"A small man does not know providence and accordingly does not fear it; he behaves saucily toward a great man; he jeers at the precepts of a sage."

## 9

The Master said, "Men born with understanding are the best; men gaining understanding through learning are next; men who manage to learn after great pains are again next; those that fail to learn even after great pains are the masses and these are the last."

## 10

The Master said, "A Man of virtue has nine things to think of: In seeing, he thinks of insight; in hearing, of discernment; in expression, of kindliness; in attitude, of humility; in speech, of sincerity; in work, of devotion; in doubt, of inquiry; in anger, of difficulties; in gain, of justice."

## 11

The Master said, " 'Hasten to copy a good act like a man dashing to catch up and shrink from an evil as from boiling water.' I saw the man living up to this precept and was thus reminded of having heard it.

" 'Go into seclusion and so achieve self-realization; live a just life and so manifest the Way of Life.' I heard this precept said but never saw the man living up to this."

## 12

The Master said, "Though Prince Ching Kung of Ch'i had four thousand horses in life, the people had nothing to praise him for, over his death. Though Po Yi and Shu Ch'i starved to death at the foot of Mt. Shou Yang, people admire them even to this day. The Book of Poems says, 'It is not wealth but distinction that is remembered.' Does it not describe that?"

## 13

Ch'en K'ang asked Po Yü, Confucius' son, "Have

you heard from the Master some special remarks such as were not told the rest?" Po Yü answered, "No, nothing special. Once as he was standing alone, I had to cross the court. He asked me, 'Have you studied the Book of Poems?' I answered, 'No, not yet.' He said, 'No one can express himself well without learning them.' So I came away and started studying the Book of Poems.

"Another day I had to cross the court again as he stood there alone. He asked, 'Have you studied the Book on Manners?' I replied, 'No, not yet.' He said, 'No man can behave with assurance without learning them.' Thereupon, I came away and started studying the Book on Manners. You see, I heard only these two things."

Ch'en K'ang went away pleased, saying, "I got three things at one question: I heard about poetry, about manners and about a virtuous man keeping his own son aloof."

# 14

A prince calls his wife lady; she calls herself little lass; her own countrymen call her princess; an envoy at a foreign court calls her petty prince; foreigners also call her princess.

# CHAPTER XVII
# Yang Ho...

## 1

Yang Ho., the notorious steward and, later, usurper of Chi, wished to see Confucius, who would not go to see him. As a device to make him come, Yang Ho sent him a pig as a gift. Choosing a time when he was not at home, Confucius paid him a formal visit of thanks. He met him, however, on the way.

Yang Ho said to Confucius, "Come, I have some talk to do with you. Should we call a man good, who, though talented, does nothing to stop state affairs going amiss?"

"No, certainly we shouldn't."

"Should we call a man intelligent, who, though enterprising, slips a good chance?"

"No, certainly not."

"Time is fleeting; the years do not stay for us."

"Good, I will get a job in the government."

## 2

The Master said, "All are akin in nature but go apart in habit."

163

### 3

The Master said, "Only the wise and the fools never move."

### 4

When the Master came to Wu Ch'eng and heard a chorus accompanied by stringed instruments, he broke into smile, saying, "Why should a cleaver be used in killing a chicken?"

Tzu Yu, the magistrate of Wu Ch'eng, responded, "This is what I heard from you formerly: 'When a great man is devoted to culture, he loves humanity; when a small man is devoted to culture, he becomes easy to use.'"

The Master said, "My young friends, Yen (Tzu Yu's personal name) is right. What I said was a joke."

### 5

Sent for by Kung Shan Fu Jao who was in revolt at Pi, Confucius had some mind to go. Tzu Lu said, displeased, "Of course, there is no question of your going. Why should you go to Kung Shan out of all people?"

The Master said, "Will anyone ask me to come for nothing? If anyone uses me, I will create an eastern Chou."

## 6

Asked by Tzu Chang about goodness, Confucius said, "To practise five things in all situations will be goodness." Asked what they were, he said, "They are humility, tolerance, faithfulness, assiduity and charity. Humble, you will not be insulted; tolerant, you will have many followers; faithful, you will be trusted; assiduous, you will achieve things; charitable, you will then be able to use people."

## 7

When the Master was inclined to go, invited by Pi Hsi of Chin Kingdom, Tzu Lu said, "Formerly, I heard you say, 'A great man never joins a bad man's group, no matter how kindly he may have been treated by him.' Then how is it that you wish to go to Pi Hsi who is in revolt at Chung Mou?"

The Master said, "True, I said that. But it is also said: 'How hard! It is never ground thin.' 'How white! It is never dyed black.' Am I a gourd to be hung and not to be eaten?"

## 8

The Master said, "Yu, have you heard six remarks on six attendant evils?"

"No, indeed."

"Sit down. I will tell you. The attendant evil of love of good without love of learning is foolishness; that of love of intelligence without love of learning is dissipation; that of love of fidelity without love of learning is disastrousness; that of love of honesty without love of learning is narrowness; that of love of courage without love of learning is violence; that of love of straightness without love of learning is extremeness."

## 9

The Master said, "My little ones, why don't you study the Book of Poems? Poetry will stir you up; it will sharpen your observation; it will make you gregarious; it will make you complain; it will help you serve your father at home and your prince far-away; it will enable you to know the names of many birds, beasts, grasses and trees."

## 10

The Master said to Po Yü, his son, "Have you

done Section Chou Nan and Section Chao Nan of the Book of Poems? A man who has not read them feels as if he were standing facing the wall."

# 11

The Master said, "They mention manners every now and then. Do they mean only jade and silk? So do they music. Does it mean only bells and drums?"

# 12

The Master said, "A man of station who is dignified outwardly but craven inwardly is like, in terms of a small man, a house-breaking thief."

# 13

The Master said, "A country gentleman who makes a point of pleasing everybody is an enemy to virtue."

# 14

The Master said, "Gossiping undermines virtue."

## 15

The Master said, "How can one bear to serve the prince side by side with a depraved fellow? When out of position, he is anxious to get one. Getting one, he is again anxious not to lose it. Once anxious not to lose his position, he will stop at nothing."

## 16

The Master said, "The ancients had three shortcomings but people in these days even lack them. The extreme of old were reckless but they are licentious nowadays; the proud of old were scrupulous but they are browbeating nowadays; the fools of old were blunt but they are deceitful nowadays."

## 17

The Master said, "I hate violet as encroaching upon vermilion, songs of Cheng as adulterating the classical music and the clever tongue as overturning the state."

## 18

The Master said, "I am going to say nothing."

Tzu Kung said, "If you do not speak, what can I write down for posterity?" The Master said, "What does Heaven say? Yet the four seasons rotate and all creatures are born. What does Heaven say?"

## 19

Ju Pei sought to see Confucius, who refused to comply on the pretext of illness. When the errand boy went out to convey the message, Confucius took up his cither and sang to its tune, letting the unwelcome visitor hear it.

## 20

Asking whether three years was not too long for a mourning period, Tsai Wo said, "If a man of station abstains from manners three years, they will fall into desuetude; if he abstains from music three years, it will be forgotten. Old grain used up, new grain comes into consumption. Wood is drilled for the renewal of the source-fire, thus a full round of changes taking place within one year. So, it seems, one year is enough for mourning."

The Master said, "Do you take comfort in eating rice and wearing silk?" Tsai Wo replied, "Yes, I do." The Master continued, "If you feel comfortable,

take them. During the mourning period, a man of
virtue, however, feels no joy in eating delicious food,
no delight in hearing music and no comfort amid
usual amenities, and consequently abstains from them.
Now you feel happy instead. Then, have them."

When Tsai Wo was gone, the Master said, "How
ungrateful Yü(Tsai Wo's personal name)is! It is
only after the lapse of three years from its birth
that a baby leaves its parents' lap. The three-year
mourning is a universal practice. Yü, too, must have
had his parents fondle him three years!"

## 21

The Master said, "If a man, glutted all day, has
nothing to occupy himself, there is no hope for him.
Is there not such thing as chess? Even to play it is
better than not."

## 22

When Tzu Lu inquired whether a great man made
much of courage, the Master said, "For a great man,
justice is to be valued most. If he has courage but
no justice, he will disturb peace. If a small man
has courage but no justice, he will become a thief."

## 23

When Tzu Kung asked whether a man of virtue, too, had hatreds, the Master answered, "Yes, he has. He hates those who are fond of pointing out others' flaws; he hates those that vilify their superiors; he hates those who have courage but no manners; he hates those who are headlong in action, not knowing what to do next."

Tzu Kung said, "I, too, have my own hatreds: l hate those who take prying for knowing, those who take insolence for courage and those who take muck-raking for frankness."

## 24

The Master said, "Only women and small men are difficult to deal with. Treated intimately, they become saucy. Kept at an arm's length, they sulk."

## 25

The Master said, "It is all up with a man who, even in his forties, is held in universal aversion."

# CHAPTER XVIII

## Wei Tzu...

### 1

Wei Tzu left the country; Ki Tzu was imprisoned as a slave; Pi Kan kept expostulating with the King until he was put to death.

The Master said, "The Yin Dynasty had three good men."

### 2

Liu Hsia Hui was dismissed three times as prison warden. Someone said to him, "Can you not leave the country for another?" He replied, "If I serve people with uprightness, where shall I not get dismissed three times? If I have to serve them in a corrupt manner, why should I leave the country of my parents?"

### 3

Prince Ching Kung of Ch'i said on the treatment he was contemplating for Confucius, "I cannot give him the same treatment as is conferred on Chi in

172

Lu, but I will give him some intermediate status between Chi and Meng." He added, "I am too old to see through all the reforms he advocates. I can not use him." Confucius left.

## 4

The men of Ch'i sent a group of dancing girls to Lu with a view to corrupting its high officials and thereby sapping its strength whose continued growth they had regarded as threatening. Chi Huan Tzu, the most powerful colleague of Confucius, accepted them. As a result, no Court was held three days. Confucius left.

## 5

A mad man of Ch'u came toward Confucius' carriage and sang as he passed, "Phoenix! Phoenix! How your virtue has declined! The past need not be fouhd fault with but the future can still be saved. Stop it all! An official career involves danger in these days."

Confucius alighted, wanting to talk with the man. But he trotted away, giving Confucius no chance.

## 6

Ch'ang Chü and Chieh Ni were tilling side by side.

Riding past, Confucius asked Tzu Lu to inquire of them about the ford. Ch'ang Chü asked, "Who is that man holding the reins?" Tzu Lu answered, "It is Kung Ch'iu. "

"Is he Kung Ch'iu of Lu?"

"Yes. "

"He knows the ford. "

Tzu Lu turned to Chieh Ni for the information. He asked, "Who are you?"

"I am Chung Yu. "

"Are you a follower of Kung Ch'iu?"

"Yes, I am. "

"The whole world is flowing down, down like this river. Who will change it? Moreover, how can following a person who avoids people compare with following us who avoid the world itself?" They went on tilling side by side.

When Tzu Lu told him all this, the Master said wistfully, "We can not herd with birds and beasts. Whom should we deal with, if not with those deprecated people? If the world were on the right path, I would not think of changing it, either. "

7

Tzu Lu, lagging behind, met an old man shouldering a bamboo basket by means of a stick and asked him, "Have you seen the Master?" The old man replied, "You mean a man who never moves his limbs in useful labor and who can not tell the five species of grain from one another? Who is a master?" He planted his stick and started hoeing.

Tzu Lu stood with his hands respectfully clasped before him. The old man detained Tzu Lu for the night, treating him to chicken and cake-millet and showing him his two sons.

The next day Tzu Lu told the story to Confucius when he found him. The Master said, "He is a hermit." He let Tzu Lu look for him. But he had already gone when Tsu Lu arrived.

Tzu Lu said, "It is not right to withhold service from the prince. If the correct behavior of youth toward their elders cannot well be demolished, far less should our allegiance to the prince be ignored. In trying to keep oneself clean, one is apt to fall into the wrong of discarding a prime duty. Great men seek government service from a sense of duty. They already know that the Way of Life will not prevail in the current world."

## 8

Voluntary outcasts were Po Yi, Shu Ch'i, Wu

Chung, Yi Yi, Chu Chang, Liu Hsia Hui and Shao Lien.

The Master said, "It was Po Yi and Shu Ch'i that did not stoop to compromise their integrity and disgrace their person. Though Liu Hsia Hui and Shao Lien compromised their integrity and disgraced their person in a way, their words fitted into moral dictums and their conducts were appropriate. They never deviated from this stand. Wu Chung and Yi Yi lived in seclusion and spoke unrestrainedly, but their behavior did not mar their purity and their negativism showed a happy balance. I am different, however, from all these. I have no set pattern. I just react as things come."

9

Grand Master of Music Chih of Lu went to Ch'i; Kan, playing for the second meal, went to Ch'u; Liao, for the third meal, to Ts'ai; Chüeh, for the fourth meal, to Ch'in; Drummer Fang Shu went to live in Ho Nei; tiny-drum-twirling Wu went to live in Han Chung; Assistant Master of Music Yang and stone-gongs-playing Hsiang went to live on an island in the sea.

## 10

Prince Chou Kung said to Prince Lu Kung, "A great man never gives away government positions to his own kin as favors; he never lets state ministers justly complain that they are too much controlled to discharge their duties with responsibility; he sees that no career man is dismissed without a serious malfeasance; he does not expect his men to be perfect in every way."

## 11

The Chou Dynasty had eight gifted subjects. They were Po Ta, Po Kuo, Chung Tu, Chung Hu, Shu Yeh, Shu Hsia, Chi Sui and Chi Kua.

# CHAPTER XIX
## Tzu Chang...

### 1

Tzu Chang said, "If a gentleman lays his life down in a crisis, thinks of justice in the face of gain, is pious in a memorial service and feels sorrow in mourning, he is indeed a worthy one."

### 2

Tzu Chang said, "If a man fails to keep his virtue all-inclusive and his faith in the Truth profound, he cannot be said to have learning, nor can he be said to have none."

### 3

When a follower of Tzu Hsia asked Tzu Chang about association, he asked in return, "What does Tzu Hsia say on it?" He answered, "Tzu Hsia says, 'Associate with the worthy but reject the unworthy.'" Thereupon, Tzu Chang said, "That is different from what I heard on the subject: 'A man of virtue treats the good with reverence while he tolerates all; he praises the able while he commiserates the inept.' If I am good enough, what people can I not tolerate? If I am not good, people will reject me. How can I have the chance to reject them?"

### 4

Tzu Hsia said, "Even small ways of life such as crafts are bound to contain some knowledge worth knowing, but a man of virtue does not take to them for fear that he will get stuck with them so as to be hindered from attaining the profundity of learning."

### 5

Tzu Hsia said, "If a man daily knows a little of what he did not and checks every month what he has already mastered, he may be called a lover of learning."

### 6

Tzu Hsia said, "If a man widens his culture and intensifies his devotion, inquires into what immediately concerns his morals and weighs things in terms of what he finds in himself, goodness will be his with no effort. "

## 7

Tzu Hsia said, "As all sorts of craftsmen master their arts in their respective shops, so a man of virtue attains the Truth through learning. "

## 8

Tzu Hsia said, "When a small man has committed a fault, he always glosses over it. "

## 9

Tzu Hsia said, "A great man changes three times. When seen from afar, he looks forbidding; when approached, he looks mild and kindly; when listened to, he is formidable. "

## 10

Tzu Hsia said, "A great man makes the people work only when trusted by them. Otherwise, they think they are oppressed. He remonstrates with the prince only when trusted by him. Otherwise, he thinks he is criticized. "

## 11

Tzu Hsia said, "Cardinal virtues are immutable, while nonessential ones can allow of flexibility. "

## 12

Tzu Yu said, "The followers of Tzu Hsia are passable in cleaning, responding to their elders and coming and going in their presence. These are, however, nonessentials. If they are taken for essentials, it is hopeless. "

On hearing this, Tzu Hsia said, "Why, Yu said wrong. In inculcating the moral precepts, how can partiality be shown, some given priority and others pushed back in negligence? Grading pupils is like classifying trees, large and small, in terms of timber. How could one misrepresent the moral precepts like that, taking nonessentials for essentials? It is only sages that start with nonessentials and finish with essentials. "

## 13

Tzu Hsia said, "Learn when your service in the

government leaves you some surplus energy; serve in the government when learning leaves you some surplus energy. "

## 14

Tzu Yu said, "The point in mourning is to be sorrowful and remain so. "

## 15

Tzu Yu said, "My friend Chang can manage difficult things and yet he is not good. "

## 16

Tseng Tzu said, "How very splendid Chang looks! It is hard, however, to admit that he is good, too. "

## 17

Tseng Tzu said, "I heard the Master say, 'If there is an involuntary thing for a man, it must be the mourning for his parents.' "

## 18

Tseng Tzu said, "I heard the Master say, 'In regard

to Meng Chuang Tzu's filial piety, we can easily copy all its aspects except this: He did not dismiss any assistant who had served his father, nor did he change what his father had instituted.'"

## 19

When appointed prison warden by Meng, Yang Fu asked Tseng Tzu's opinion. He replied, "Under a lawless leadership, the people have long been demoralized. If you knew your prisoners' backgrounds, you would be inclined to commiserate rather than gloat over them."

## 20

Tzu Kung said, "Chou, the Tyrant, was not so evil as he has been represented to be. That is why a gentleman hates degradation in any form. Once degraded, he will get all the evils in the world heaped upon himself."

## 21

Tzu Kung said, "A great man's faults are like solar or lunar eclipses. All see them when they occur. When they are mended, all look up."

## 22

State Minister Kung Sun Ch'ao of Wei asked Tzu Kung how Chung Ni (Confucius' pen name) had learned. Tzu Kung replied, "The ways of King Won and King Wu have not fallen to the ground but are always conveyed in men. The wise understanding great ways and the unwise small ways, none are without some of them. How could the Master help learning from all he came across? But what particular teacher did he ever study under?"

## 23

Shu Sun Wu Shu told all the ministers at Court that Tzu Kung was wiser than Chung Ni. When Tzu Fu Ching Po informed Tzu Kung of this, he said, "Compared to walls, I am like a shoulder-high one that permits the pretty house to be peeped into from outside. The Master is like one many human lengths high. Unless a man gets in through the gate, he cannot see the beautiful royal shrine and rank upon rank of resplendent officials. Few have entered the gate. No wonder he talked that way."

## 24

Shu Sun Wu Shu spoke evil of Chung Ni. Tzu

Kung said, "Chung Ni is not to be slandered. Other
sages are like climbable hills, but Chung Ni is unapproachable like the sun or the moon that can not
be reached. Even though a man rejects him, it will
not affect him. Will a man's keeping away from
the sun and the moon affect them? It will only reveal his own lack of comprehension. "

## 25

Ch'en Tzu Ch'in said to Tzu Kung, "That is your
modesty. How can Chung Ni be wiser than you?"
Tzu Kung replied, "One word from a gentleman
reveals his wisdom or ignorance. So speech cannot be
too careful. The Master is unapproachable just as the
sky is unreachable by flights of steps. Were he placed
at the helm of a government, the people would
stand, bidden, go, led, come, comforted, and be
welded, moved. His life would have been glorious;
his death lamented with sorrow. How could we hope
to approach him?"

# CHAPTER XX
## The Emperor Yao...

### 1

The Emperor Yao made this proclamation on the occasion of abdicating for Shun: "Behold, Shun! Heaven's favor is on you. Hold fast to the golden mean. Remember that, if the people become poverty-stricken, the means of the reigning house will come to an end."

Shun also made the same proclamation when he abdicated in the interest of Yü.

On deposing Chieh, the Tyrant, T'ang made this proclamation: "I Li (T'ang's personal name), Thine little child, with the offering of a black bull, humbly address this to Thee: 'The guilty I dare not pardon but Thine subjects shall not be neglected. I know this is to Thy mind. My guilts should not be imputed to the people. But the blame of the guilts among the people should be laid on my person.'"

The Chou Dynasty distributed largesses throughout the empire, but it was only the good that prospered.

King Wu's proclamation says in part, "The nearest kin are not so helpful as good men. When the people commit guilts, their blame should be laid on me."

Measures were uniformalized; laws and institutions were adapted anew; closed offices were manned again. Thus administration was efficient in all places.

Submerged nations were revived; broken family lines were renewed; talented people whom misrule had driven into seclusion were elevated. Consequently, there was an upsurge of popular enthusiasm for the new dynasty.

The sustenance, mourning and memorial service of the people were regarded most essential.

Generosity makes for large following; faithfulness inspires popular confidence; assiduity leads to achievements; fairness evokes general gratification.

## 2

When, Tzu Chang inquired how one could be a successful administrator, the Master answered, "To value five merits and avoid four evils would make an administrator successful." When Tzu Chang again asked what were the five merits, the Master said, "A great man is charitable but not wasteful, toiling without complaining, ambitious but not avaricious, weighty but not haughty, dignified but not terrifying." Further explanation requested, the Master said, "Profiting people by letting them do profitable things themselves, can he help being charitable without waste? Toiling where toiling is called for, against whom is he to complain? Ambitious of good work and getting it done, how can he also be avaricious? Single-minded in everything, whether large or small, whether concerning many or few, can he be otherwise than weighty but not haughty? Neat in dress, looking straight ahead and deporting himself with such gravity as to inspire awe, can he but be dignified without being terrible?"

Asked by Tzu Chang, then, what were four evils, the Master said, "Killing without teaching is called tyranny; exacting achievement without instruction is called arbitrariness; to have a belated order complied with within the specified time is called robbery; to give grudgingly what has been earmarked for the people is called pettiness."

## 3

The Master said, "One cannot be a great man without knowing providence; one cannot behave with confidence without knowing manners; one cannot know people without knowing their words."

# 目　次

# 一. 學 而

（1）　子曰學而時習之不亦說乎有朋自遠方來不亦樂乎
人不知而不慍不亦君子乎。

（2）　有子曰其為人也孝弟而好犯上者鮮矣不好犯上而
好作亂者未之有也。君子務本本立而道生孝弟也者其為
仁之本與。

（3）　子曰巧言令色鮮矣仁。

（4）　曾子曰吾日三省吾身為人謀而不忠乎與朋友交而
不信乎傳不習乎。

（5）　子曰道千乘之國敬事而信節用而愛人使民以時。

（6）　子曰弟子入則孝出則悌謹而信汎愛眾而親仁行有
餘力則以學文。

（7）　子夏曰賢賢易色事父母能竭其力事君能致其身與
朋友交言而有信雖曰未學吾必謂之學矣。

（8）　子曰君子不重則不威學則不固。主忠信無友不如
己者過則勿憚改。

（9）　曾子曰慎終追遠民德歸厚矣。

（10）　子禽問於子貢曰夫子至於是邦也必聞其政求之與
抑與之與。子貢曰夫子溫良恭儉讓以得之夫子之求之也

其諸異乎人之求之與。

（11） 子曰父在觀其志父沒觀其行三年無改於父之道可謂孝矣。

（12） 有子曰禮之用和爲貴先王之道斯爲美小大由之。有所不行知和而和不以禮節之亦不可行也。

（13） 有子曰信近於義言可復也恭近於禮遠恥辱也因不失其親亦可宗也。

（14） 子曰君子食無求飽居無求安敏於事而慎於言就有道而正焉可謂好學也已。

（15） 子貢曰貧而無諂富而無驕何如。子曰可也未若貧而樂富而好禮者也。子貢曰詩云如切如磋如琢如磨其斯之謂與。子曰賜也始可與言詩已矣告諸往而知來者。

（16） 子曰不患人之不己知患不知人也。

## 二. 爲　政

（1） 子曰爲政以德譬如北辰居其所而衆星共之。

（2） 子曰詩三百一言以蔽之曰思無邪。

（3） 子曰道之以政齊之以刑民免而無恥。道之以德齊之以禮有恥且格。

（4） 子曰吾十有五而志于學三十而立四十而不惑五十

而知天命六十而耳順七十而從心所欲不踰矩。

（5）　孟懿子問孝子曰無違。樊遲御子告之曰孟孫問孝於我我對曰無違。樊遲曰何謂也子曰生事之以禮死葬之以禮祭之以禮。

（6）　孟武伯問孝子曰父母唯其疾之憂

（7）　子游問孝子曰今之孝者是謂能養至於犬馬皆能有養不敬何以別乎。

（8）　子夏問孝子曰色難有事弟子服其勞有酒食先生饌曾是以爲孝乎。

（9）　子曰吾與回言終日不違如愚退而省其私亦足以發回也不愚。

（10）　子曰視其所以觀其所由察其所安人焉廋哉人焉廋哉。

（11）　子曰溫故而知新可以爲師矣。

（12）　子曰君子不器。

（13）　子貢問君子子曰先行其言而後從之。

（14）　子曰君子周而不比小人比而不周。

（15）　子曰學而不思則罔思而不學則殆。

（16）　子曰攻乎異端斯害也已。

（17）　子曰由誨女知之乎知之爲知之不知爲不知是知也。

194

(18)　子張學干祿子曰多聞闕疑愼言其餘則寡尤多見闕殆愼行其餘則寡悔言寡尤行寡悔祿在其中矣。

(19)　哀公問曰何爲則民服。孔子對曰舉直錯諸枉則民服舉枉錯諸直則民不服。

(20)　季康子問使民敬忠以勸如之何。子曰臨之以莊則敬孝慈則忠舉善而教不能則勸。

(21)　或謂孔子曰子奚不爲政。子曰書云孝乎惟孝友于兄弟施於有政是亦爲政奚其爲爲政。

(22)　子曰人而無信不知其可也大車無輗小車無軏其何以行之哉。

(23)　子張問十世可知也。子曰殷因於夏禮所損益可知也。周因於殷禮所損益可知也其或繼周者雖百世可知也。

(24)　子曰非其鬼而祭之諂也。見義不爲無勇也。

## 三. 八　佾

（1）　孔子謂季氏八佾舞於庭是可忍也孰不可忍也。

（2）　三家者以雍徹子曰相維辟公天子穆穆奚取於三家之堂。

（3）　子曰人而不仁如禮何人而不仁如樂何。

（4）　林放問禮之本子曰大哉問禮與其奢也寧儉喪與其

易也寧戚。

（5）　子曰夷狄之有君不如諸夏之亡也。

（6）　季氏旅於泰山子謂冉有曰女不能救與對曰不能子曰嗚呼曾謂泰山不如林放乎。

（7）　子曰君子無所爭必也射乎揖讓而升下而飲其爭也君子。

（8）　子夏問曰巧笑倩兮美目盼兮素以爲絢兮何謂也。子曰繪事後素。曰禮後乎。子曰起予者商也始可與言詩已矣。

（9）　子曰夏禮吾能言之杞不足徵也殷禮吾能言之宋不足徵也文獻不足故也足則吾能徵之矣。

（10）　子曰禘自既灌而往者吾不欲觀之矣。

（11）　或問禘之說子曰不知也知其說者之於天下也其如示諸斯乎指其掌。

（12）　祭如在祭神如神在。子曰吾不與祭如不祭。

（13）　王孫賈問曰與其媚於奧寧媚於竈何謂也。子曰不然獲罪於天無所禱也。

（14）　子曰周監於二代郁郁乎文哉吾從周。

（15）　子入大廟每事問。或曰孰謂鄹人之子知禮乎入大廟每事問。子聞之曰是禮也。

(16) 子曰射不主皮爲力不同科古之道也。

(17) 子貢欲去告朔之餼羊。子曰賜也爾愛其羊我愛其禮。

(18) 子曰事君盡禮人以爲諂也。

(19) 定公問君使臣臣事君如之何。孔子對曰君使臣以禮臣事君以忠。

(20) 子曰關雎樂而不淫哀而不傷。

(21) 哀公問社於宰我宰我對曰夏后氏以松殷人以柏周人以栗曰使民戰栗。子聞之曰成事不說遂事不諫既往不咎。

(22) 子曰管仲之器小哉。或曰管仲儉乎。曰管氏有三歸官事不攝焉得儉。然則管仲知禮乎。曰邦君樹塞門管氏亦樹塞門邦君爲兩君之好有反坫管氏亦有反坫管氏而知禮孰不知禮。

(23) 子語魯大師樂曰樂其可知也始作翕如也從之純如也皦如也繹如也以成。

(24) 儀封人請見曰君子之至於斯也吾未嘗不得見也從者見之出曰二三子何患於喪乎天下之無道也久矣天將以夫子爲木鐸。

(25) 子謂韶盡美矣又盡善也謂武盡美矣未盡善也。

(26)　子曰居上不寬爲禮不敬臨喪不哀吾何以觀之哉。

## 四. 里　仁

（1）　子曰里仁爲美擇不處仁焉得知。

（2）　子曰不仁者不可以久處約不可以長處樂仁者安仁知者利仁。

（3）　子曰惟仁者能好人能惡人。

（4）　子曰苟志於仁矣無惡也。

（5）　子曰富與貴是人之所欲也不以其道得之不處也貧與賤是人之所惡也不以其道得之不去也君子去仁惡乎成名君子無終食之間違仁造次必於是顚沛必於是。

（6）　子曰我未見好仁者惡不仁者好仁者無以尙之惡不仁者其爲仁矣不使不仁者加乎其身。有能一日用其力於仁矣乎我未見力不足者。蓋有之矣我未之見也。

（7）　子曰人之過也各於其黨觀過斯知仁矣。

（8）　子曰朝聞道夕死可矣。

（9）　子曰士志於道而恥惡衣惡食者未足與議也。

（10）　子曰君子之於天下也無適也無莫也義之與比。

（11）　子曰君子懷德小人懷土君子懷刑小人懷惠。

（12）　子曰放於利而行多怨。

(13) 子曰能以禮讓爲國乎何有不能以禮讓爲國如禮何。

(14) 子曰不患無位患所以立不患莫己知求爲可知也。

(15) 子曰參乎吾道一以貫之曾子曰唯。子出門人問曰何謂也曾子曰夫子之道忠恕而已矣。

(16) 子曰君子喩於義小人喩於利。

(17) 子曰見賢思齊焉見不賢而內自省也。

(18) 子曰事父母幾諫見志不從又敬不違勞而不怨。

(19) 子曰父母在不遠遊遊必有方。

(20) 子曰父母之年不可不知也一則以喜一則以懼。

(21) 子曰古者言之不出恥躬之不逮也。

(22) 子曰以約失之者鮮矣。

(23) 子曰君子欲訥於言而敏於行。

(24) 子曰德不孤必有鄰。

(25) 子游曰事君數斯辱矣朋友數斯疏矣。

## 五. 公 冶 長

( 1 ) 子謂公冶長可妻也雖在縲絏之中非其罪也以其子妻之。

( 2 ) 子謂南容邦有道不廢邦無道免於刑戮以其兄之子妻之。

（3）　子謂子賤君子哉若人魯無君子者斯焉取斯。

（4）　子貢問曰賜也何如子曰女器也。曰何器也。曰瑚
璉也。

（5）　或曰雍也仁而不佞。子曰焉用佞禦人以口給屢憎
於人不知其仁焉用佞。

（6）　子使漆雕開仕對曰吾斯之未能信子說。

（7）　子曰道不行乘桴浮于海從我者其由與子路聞之喜。
子曰由也好勇過我無所取材。

（8）　孟武伯問子路仁乎子曰不知也又問子曰由也千乘
之國可使治其賦也不知其仁。求也何如子曰求也千室
之邑百乘之家可使爲之宰也不知其仁也。赤也何如子曰
赤也束帶立於朝可使與賓客言也不知其仁也。

（9）　子謂子貢曰女與回也孰愈。對曰賜也何敢望回回也
聞一以知十賜也聞一以知二。子曰弗如也吾與女弗如也。

（10）　宰予晝寢。子曰朽木不可雕也糞土之牆不可杇也
於予與何誅。子曰始吾於人也聽其言而信其行今吾於人
也聽其言而觀其行於予與改是。

（11）　子曰吾未見剛者。或對曰申棖。子曰棖也慾焉得
剛。

（12）　子貢曰我不欲人之加諸我也吾亦欲無加諸人。子

曰賜也非爾所及也。

(13) 子貢曰夫子之文章可得而聞也夫子之言性與天道不可得而聞也。

(14) 子路有聞未之能行唯恐有聞。

(15) 子貢問曰孔文子何以謂之文也子曰敏而好學不恥下問是以謂之文也。

(16) 子謂子產有君子之道四焉其行己也恭其事上也敬其養民也惠其使民也義。

(17) 子曰晏平仲善與人交久而敬之。

(18) 子曰臧文仲居蔡山節藻梲何如其知也。

(19) 子張問曰令尹子文三仕爲令尹無喜色三巳之無慍色舊令尹之政必以告新令尹何如。子曰忠矣。曰仁矣乎曰未知焉得仁。崔子弒齊君陳文子有馬十乘棄而違之至於他邦則曰猶吾大夫崔子也違之之一邦則又曰猶吾大夫崔子也違之何如。子曰清矣。曰仁矣乎。曰未知焉得仁。

(20) 季文子三思而後行。子聞之曰再斯可矣。

(21) 子曰甯武子邦有道則知邦無道則愚其知可及也其愚不可及也。

(22) 子在陳曰歸與歸與吾黨之小子狂簡斐然成章不知

所以裁之。

(23) 子曰伯夷叔齊不念舊惡怨是用希。

(24) 子曰孰謂微生高直或乞醯焉乞諸其鄰而與之。

(25) 子曰巧言令色足恭左丘明恥之丘亦恥之匿怨而友
其人左丘明恥之丘亦恥之。

(26) 顏淵季路侍子曰盍各言爾志。子路曰願車馬衣輕
裘與朋友共敝之而無憾。顏淵曰願無伐善無施勞。子路
曰願聞子之志。子曰老者安之朋友信之少者懷之。

(27) 子曰已矣乎吾未見能見其過而內自訟者也。

(28) 子曰十室之邑必有忠信如丘者焉不如丘之好學也。


# 六．雍　　也

（1）　子曰雍也可使南面。仲弓問子桑伯子子曰可也簡。
仲弓曰居敬而行簡以臨其民不亦可乎居簡而行簡無乃大
簡乎。子曰雍之言然。

（2）　哀公問弟子孰爲好學孔子對曰有顏回者好學不遷
怒不貳過不幸短命死矣今也則亡未聞好學者也。

（3）　子華使於齊冉子爲其母請粟子曰與之釜請益曰與
之庾冉子與之粟五秉。子曰赤之適齊也乘肥馬衣輕裘吾
聞之也君子周急不繼富。

（4）　原思爲之宰與之粟九百辭子曰毋以與爾鄰里鄉黨乎。

（5）　子謂仲弓曰犁牛之子騂且角雖欲勿用山川其舍諸。

（6）　子曰回也其心三月不違仁其餘則日月至焉而已矣。

（7）　季康子問仲由可使從政也與子曰由也果於從政乎何有曰賜也可使從政也與曰賜也達於從政乎何有曰求也可使從政也與曰求也藝於從政乎何有。

（8）　季氏使閔子騫爲費宰閔子騫曰善爲我辭焉如有復我者則吾必在汶上矣。

（9）　伯牛有疾子問之自牖執其手曰亡之命矣夫斯人也而有斯疾也斯人也而有斯疾也。

（10）　子曰賢哉回也一簞食一瓢飲在陋巷人不堪其憂回也不改其樂賢哉回也。

（11）　冉求曰非不說子之道力不足也子曰力不足者中道而廢今女畫。

（12）　子謂子夏曰女爲君子儒無爲小人儒。

（13）　子游爲武城宰子曰女得人焉爾乎曰有澹臺滅明者行不由徑非公事未嘗至於偃之室也。

（14）　子曰孟之反不伐奔而殿將入門策其馬曰非敢後也馬不進也。

(15)　子曰不有祝鮀之佞而有宋朝之美難乎免於今之世矣。

(16)　子曰誰能出不由戶何莫由斯道也。

(17)　子曰質勝文則野文勝質則史文質彬彬然後君子。

(18)　子曰人之生也直罔之生也幸而免。

(19)　子曰知之者不如好之者好之者不如樂之者。

(20)　子曰中人以上可以語上也中人以下不可以語上也。

(21)　樊遲問知子曰務民之義敬鬼神而遠之可謂知矣。問仁曰仁者先難而後獲可謂仁矣。

(22)　子曰知者樂水仁者樂山知者動仁者靜知者樂仁者壽。

(23)　子曰齊一變至於魯魯一變至於道。

(24)　子曰觚不觚觚哉觚哉。

(25)　宰我問曰仁者雖告之曰井有仁焉其從之也。子曰何爲其然也君子可逝也不可陷也可欺也不可罔也。

(26)　子曰君子博學於文約之以禮亦可以弗畔矣夫。

(27)　子見南子子路不說。夫子矢之曰予所否者天厭之天厭之。

(28)　子曰中庸之爲德也其至矣乎民鮮久矣。

(29)　子貢曰如有博施於民而能濟衆何如可謂仁乎。子曰何事於仁必也聖乎堯舜其猶病諸。夫仁者己欲立而立人己欲達而達人。能近取譬可謂仁之方也已。

## 七. 述　而

（1）　子曰述而不作信而好古竊比於我老彭。

（2）　子曰默而識之學而不厭誨人不倦何有於我哉。

（3）　子曰德之不修學之不講聞義不能徙不善不能改是吾憂也。

（4）　子之燕居申申如也夭夭如也。

（5）　子曰甚矣吾衰也久矣吾不復夢見周公。

（6）　子曰志於道。據於德。依於仁。游於藝。

（7）　子曰自行束脩以上吾未嘗無誨焉。

（8）　子曰不憤不啓不悱不發舉一隅不以三隅反則不復也。

（9）　子食於有喪者之側未嘗飽也。子於是日哭則不歌。

（10）　子謂顏淵曰用之則行舍之則藏惟我與爾有是夫。子路曰子行三軍則誰與。子曰暴虎馮河死而無悔者吾不與也必也臨事而懼好謀而成者也。

（11）　子曰富而可求也雖執鞭之士吾亦為之如不可求從吾所好。

**（12）　子之所慎齊戰疾。**

(13) 子在齊聞韶三月不知肉味曰不圖爲樂之至於斯也。

(14) 冉有曰夫子爲衛君乎子貢曰諾吾將問之。入曰伯夷叔齊何人也。曰古之賢人也。曰怨乎。曰求仁而得仁又何怨出曰夫子不爲也。

(15) 子曰飯疏食飲水曲肱而枕之樂亦在其中矣不義而富且貴於我如浮雲。

(16) 子曰加我數年五十以學易可以無大過矣。

(17) 子所雅言詩書執禮皆雅言也。

(18) 葉公問孔子於子路子路不對。子曰女奚不曰其爲人也發憤忘食樂以忘憂不知老之將至云爾。

(19) 子曰我非生而知之者好古敏以求之者也。

(20) 子不語怪力亂神。

(21) 子曰三人行必有我師焉擇其善者而從之其不善者而改之。

(22) 子曰天生德於予桓魋其如予何。

(23) 子曰二三子以我爲隱乎吾無隱乎爾吾無行而不與二三子者是丘也。

(24) 子以四教文行忠信。

(25) 子曰聖人吾不得而見之矣得見君子者斯可矣。子曰善人吾不得而見之矣得見有恒者斯可矣。亡而爲有虛而爲盈約而爲泰難乎有恒矣。

(26)　子釣而不網弋不射宿。

(27)　子曰蓋有不知而作之者我無是也多聞擇其善者而從之多見而識之知之次也。

(28)　互鄉難與言童子見門人惑。子曰人潔己以進與其潔也不保其往也與其進也不與其退也唯何甚。

(29)　子曰仁遠乎哉我欲仁斯仁至矣。

(30)　陳司敗問昭公知禮乎孔子曰知禮。孔子退揖巫馬期而進之曰吾聞君子不黨君子亦黨乎君取於吳爲同姓謂之吳孟子君而知禮孰不知禮。巫馬期以告子曰丘也幸苟有過人必知之。

(31)　子與人歌而善必使反之而後和之。

(32)　子曰文莫吾猶人也躬行君子則吾未之有得。

(33)　子曰若聖與仁則吾豈敢抑爲之不厭誨人不倦則可謂云爾已矣公西華曰正唯弟子不能學也。

(34)　子疾病子路請禱子曰有諸子路對曰有之誄曰禱爾于上下神祇子曰丘之禱久矣。

(35)　子曰奢則不孫儉則固與其不孫也寧固。

(36)　子曰君子坦蕩蕩小人長戚戚。

**(37)**　子溫而厲威而不猛恭而安。

## 八．泰　伯

（１）　子曰泰伯其可謂至德也已矣三以天下讓民無得而稱焉。

（２）　子曰恭而無禮則勞愼而無禮則葸勇而無禮則亂直而無禮則絞。

（３）　君子篤於親則民興於仁故舊不遺則民不偸。

（４）　曾子有疾召門弟子曰啓予足啓予手詩云戰戰兢兢如臨深淵如履薄冰而今而後吾知免夫小子。

（５）　曾子有疾孟敬子問之曾子言曰鳥之將死其鳴也哀人之將死其言也善。君子所貴乎道者三動容貌斯遠暴慢矣正顏色斯近信矣出辭氣斯遠鄙倍矣籩豆之事則有司存。

（６）　曾子曰以能問於不能以多問於寡有若無實若虛犯而不校昔者吾友嘗從事於斯矣。

（７）　曾子曰可以託六尺之孤可以寄百里之命臨大節而不可奪也君子人與君子人也。

（８）　曾子曰士不可以不弘毅任重而道遠。仁以爲己任不亦重乎死而後已不亦遠乎。

（９）　子曰興於詩立於禮成於樂。

（１０）　子曰民可使由之不可使知之。

(11) 子曰好勇疾貧亂也人而不仁疾之已甚亂也。

(12) 子曰如有周公之才之美使驕且吝其餘不足觀也已。

(13) 子曰三年學不至於穀不易得也。

(14) 子曰篤信好學守死善道。危邦不入亂邦不居天下
有道則見無道則隱。邦有道貧且賤焉恥也邦無道富且貴
焉恥也。

(15) 子曰不在其位不謀其政。

(16) 子曰師摯之始關雎之亂洋洋乎盈耳哉。

(17) 子曰狂而不直侗而不愿悾悾而不信吾不知之矣。

(18) 子曰學如不及猶恐失之。

(19) 子曰巍巍乎舜禹之有天下也而不與焉。

(20) 子曰大哉堯之為君也巍巍乎唯天為大唯堯則之蕩
蕩乎民無能名焉。巍巍乎其有成功也煥乎其有文章。

(21) 舜有臣五人而天下治。武王曰予有亂臣十人。孔
子曰才難不其然乎唐虞之際於斯為盛有婦人焉九人而已。
三分天下有其二以服事殷周之德其可謂至德也已矣。

(22) 子曰禹吾無間然矣菲飲食而致孝乎鬼神惡衣服而
致美乎黻冕卑宮室而盡力乎溝洫禹吾無間然矣。

## 九 子 罕

（1） 子罕言利與命與仁。

（2） 達巷黨人曰大哉孔子博學而無所成名。子聞之謂
門弟子曰吾何執執御乎執射乎吾執御矣。

（3） 子曰麻冕禮也今也純儉吾從衆。拜下禮也今拜乎
上泰也雖違衆吾從下。

（4） 子絕四毋意毋必毋固毋我。

（5） 子畏於匡。曰文王旣沒文不在兹乎天之將喪斯文
也後死者不得與於斯文也天之未喪斯文也匡人其如予何.

（6） 太宰問於子貢曰夫子聖者與何其多能也。子貢曰
固天縱之將聖又多能也。子聞之曰太宰知我乎吾少也賤
故多能鄙事君子多乎哉不多也。牢曰子云吾不試故藝。

（7） 子曰吾有知乎哉無知也有鄙夫問於我空空如也我
叩其兩端而竭焉。

（8） 子曰鳳鳥不至河不出圖吾已矣夫。

（9） 子見齊衰者冕衣裳者與瞽者見之雖少必作。過之
必趨。

（10） 顏淵喟然歎曰仰之彌高鑽之彌堅瞻之在前忽焉在
後。夫子循循然善誘人博我以文約我以禮。欲罷不能旣

竭吾才如有所立卓爾雖欲從之末由也已。

(11) 子疾病子路使門人爲臣。病間曰久矣哉由之行詐
也無臣而爲有臣吾誰欺欺天乎。且予與其死於臣之手也
無寧死於二三子之手乎且予縱不得大葬予死於道路乎。

(12) 子貢曰有美玉於斯韞匱而藏諸求善賈而沽諸子曰
沽之哉沽之哉我待賈者也。

(13) 子欲居九夷。或曰陋如之何。子曰君子居之何陋
之有。

(14) 子曰吾自衛反魯然後樂正雅頌各得其所。

(15) 子曰出則事公卿入則事父兄喪事不敢不勉不爲酒
困何有於我哉。

(16) 子在川上曰逝者如斯夫不舍晝夜。

(17) 子曰吾未見好德如好色者也。

(18) 子曰譬如爲山未成一簣止吾止也譬如平地雖覆一
簣進吾往也。

(19) 子曰語之而不惰者其回也與。

(20) 子謂顏淵曰惜乎吾見其進也未見其止也。

(21) 子苗而不秀者有矣夫秀而不實者有矣夫。

(22) 子曰後生可畏焉知來者之不如今也四十五十而無
聞焉斯亦不足畏也已,

(23)　子曰法語之言能無從乎改之爲貴巽與之言能無說乎繹之爲貴說而不繹從而不改吾末如之何也已矣。

(24)　子曰三軍可奪帥也匹夫不可奪志也。

(25)　子曰衣敝縕袍與衣狐貉者立而不恥者其由也與。不忮不求何用不臧。子路終身誦之。子曰是道也何足以臧。

(26)　子曰歲寒然後知松柏之後彫也。

(27)　子曰知者不惑仁者不憂勇者不懼。

(28)　子曰可與共學未可與適道可與適道未可與立可與立未可與權。

(29)　唐棣之華偏其反而豈不爾思室是遠而。子曰未之思也夫何遠之有。


# 十　鄉　黨

（1）　孔子於鄉黨恂恂如也似不能言者。其在宗廟朝廷便便言唯謹爾。

（2）　朝與下大夫言侃侃如也與上大夫言誾誾如也。君在踧踖如也與與如也。

（3）　君召使擯色勃如也足躩如也。揖所與立左右手衣

212

前後襜如也。趨進翼如也。賓退必復命曰賓不顧矣。

（4） 入公門鞠躬如也如不容。立不中門行不履閾。過位色勃如也足躩如也其言似不足者。攝齊升堂鞠躬如也屏氣似不息者。出降一等逞顏色怡怡如也沒階趨翼如也復其位踧踖如也。

（5） 執圭鞠躬如也如不勝上如揖下如授勃如戰色足蹜蹜如有循。享禮有容色。私覿愉愉如也。

（6） 君子不以紺緅飾紅紫不以爲褻服。當暑袗絺綌必表而出之。緇衣羔裘素衣麑裘黃衣狐裘。褻裘長短右袂。必有寢衣長一身有半。狐貉之厚以居。去喪無所不佩。非帷裳必殺之。羔裘玄冠不以弔。吉月必朝服而朝。

（7） 齊必有明衣布。齊必變食居必遷坐。

（8） 食不厭精膾不厭細。食饐而餲魚餒而肉敗不食色惡不食臭惡不食失飪不食不時不食。割不正不食不得其醬不食。肉雖多不使勝食氣。惟酒無量不及亂。沽酒市脯不食。不撤薑食。不多食。祭於公不宿肉祭肉不出三日出三日不食之矣。食不語寢不言。雖疏食菜羹瓜祭必齊如也。

（9） 席不正不坐。

（10） 鄉人飲酒杖者出斯出矣。鄉人儺朝服而立於阼階。

(11) 問人於他邦再拜而送之。康子饋藥拜而受之曰丘未達不敢嘗。

(12) 廐焚子退朝曰傷人乎不問馬。

(13) 君賜食必正席先嘗之。君賜腥必熟而薦之君賜生必畜之。侍食於君君祭先飯。疾君視之東首加朝服拖紳。君命召不俟駕行矣。

(14) 朋友死無所歸曰於我殯。朋友之饋雖車馬非祭肉不拜。

(15) 寢不尸居不容。見齊衰者雖狎必變見冕者與瞽者雖褻必以貌。凶服者式之式負版者。有盛饌必變色而作。迅雷風烈必變。

(16) 升車必正立執綏。車中不內顧不疾言不親指。

(17) 色斯舉矣翔而後集。曰山梁雌雉時哉時哉子路共之三嗅而作。


## 十一. 先　　進

（1） 子曰先進於禮樂野人也後進於禮樂君子也。如用之則吾從先進。

（2） 子曰從我於陳蔡者皆不及門也德行顏淵閔子騫冉

伯牛仲弓言語宰我子貢政事冉有季路文學子游子夏。

（3）　子曰回也非助我者也於吾言無所不說。

（4）　子曰孝哉閔子騫人不間於其父母昆弟之言。

（5）　南容三復白圭孔子以其兄之子妻之。

（6）　季康子問弟子孰爲好學孔子對曰有顏回者好學
不幸短命死矣今也則亡。

（7）　顏淵死顏路請子之車以爲之椁。子曰才不才亦各
言其子也鯉也死有棺而無椁吾不徒行以爲之椁以吾從大
夫之後不可徒行也。

（8）　顏淵死子曰噫天喪予天喪予。

（9）　顏淵死子哭之慟從者曰子慟矣。曰有慟乎非夫人
之爲慟而誰爲。

（10）　顏淵死門人欲厚葬之子曰不可門人厚葬之。子曰
回也視予猶父也予不得視猶子也非我也夫二三子也。

（11）　季路問事鬼神子曰未能事人焉能事鬼。敢問死曰
未知生焉知死。

（12）　閔子侍側誾誾如也子路行行如也冉有子貢侃侃如
也子樂。若由也不得其死然。

（13）　魯人爲長府閔子騫曰仍舊貫如之何何必改作。子
曰夫人不言言必有中。

(14) 子曰由之瑟奚爲於丘之門。門人不敬子路子曰由也升堂矣未入於室也。

(15) 子貢問師與商也孰賢子曰師也過商也不及。曰然則師愈與。子曰過猶不及。

(16) 季氏富於周公而求也爲之聚斂而附益之。子曰非吾徒也小子鳴鼓而攻之可也。

(17) 柴也愚參也魯師也辟由也喭。子曰回也其庶乎屢空。賜不受命而貨殖焉億則屢中。

(18) 子張問善人之道子曰不踐迹亦不入於室。

(19) 子曰論篤是與君子者乎色莊者乎。

(20) 子路問聞斯行諸子曰有父兄在如之何其聞斯行之。冉有問聞斯行諸子曰聞斯行之公西華曰由也問聞斯行諸子曰有父兄在求也問聞斯行諸子曰聞斯行之赤也惑敢問子曰求也退故進之由也兼人故退之。

(21) 子畏於匡顏淵後子曰吾以女爲死矣曰子在回何敢死。

(22) 季子然問仲由冉求可謂大臣與。子曰吾以子爲異之問曾由與求之問。所謂大臣者以道事君不可則止今由與求也可謂具臣矣。曰然則從之者與。子曰弑父與君亦不從也。

(23) 子路使子羔爲費宰子曰賊夫人之子。子路曰有民
人焉有社稷焉何必讀書然後爲學。子曰是故惡夫佞者。

(24) 子路曾皙冉有公西華侍坐子曰以吾一日長乎爾毋
吾以也。居則曰不吾知也如或知爾則何以哉。子路率爾
而對曰千乘之國攝乎大國之間加之以師旅因之以饑饉由
也爲之比及三年可使有勇且知方也夫子哂之。求爾何如
對曰方六七十如五六十 求也爲之比及三年可使足民如
其禮樂以俟君子。赤爾何如對曰非曰能之願學焉宗廟之
事如會同端章甫願爲小相焉。點爾何如鼓瑟希鏗爾舍瑟
而作對曰異乎三子者之撰子曰何傷乎亦各言其志也曰莫
春者春服既成冠者五六人童子六七人浴乎沂風乎舞雩詠
而歸夫子喟然歎曰吾與點也。三子者出曾皙後曾皙曰夫
三子者之言何如子曰亦各言其志也已矣。曰夫子何哂由
也。曰爲國以禮其言不讓是故哂之。唯求則非邦也與。
安見方六七十如五六十而非邦也者。唯赤則非邦也與。
宗廟會同非諸侯而何赤也爲之小孰能爲之大。

## 十二. 顏 淵

（1） 顏淵問仁子曰克己復禮爲仁一日克己復禮天下歸
仁焉爲仁由己而由人乎哉。顏淵曰請問其目子曰非禮勿

視非禮勿聽非禮勿言非禮勿動顏淵曰回雖不敏請事斯語矣。

（2） 仲弓問仁子曰出門如見大賓使民如承大祭已所不欲勿施於人在邦無怨在家無怨仲弓曰雍雖不敏請事斯語矣。

（3） 司馬牛問仁子曰仁者其言也訒。曰其言也訒斯謂之仁矣乎子曰爲之難言之得無訒乎。

（4） 司馬牛問君子子曰君子不憂不懼。曰不憂不懼斯謂之君子矣乎子曰內省不疚夫何憂何懼。

（5） 司馬牛憂曰人皆有兄弟我獨亡。子夏曰商聞之矣死生有命富貴在天。君子敬而無失與人恭而有禮四海之內皆兄弟也君子何患乎無兄弟也。

（6） 子張問明子曰浸潤之譖膚受之愬不行焉可謂明也已矣浸潤之譖膚受之愬不行焉可謂遠也已矣。

（7） 子貢問政子曰足食足兵民信之矣。子貢曰必不得已而去於斯三者何先曰去兵。子貢曰必不得已而去於斯二者何先曰去食自古皆有死民無信不立。

（8） 棘子成曰君子質而已矣何以文爲。子貢曰惜乎夫子之說君子也駟不及舌文猶質也質猶文也虎豹之鞟猶犬羊之鞟。

218

（9）　哀公問於有若曰年饑用不足如之何。有若對曰盍
徹乎。曰二吾猶不足如之何其徹也。對曰百姓足君孰與
不足百姓不足君孰與足。

（10）　子張問崇德辨惑子曰主忠信徙義崇德也。愛之欲
其生惡之欲其死既欲其生又欲其死是惑也。

（11）　齊景公問政於孔子孔子對曰君君臣臣父父子子。
公曰善哉信如君不君臣不臣父不父子不子雖有粟吾得而
食諸。

（12）　子曰片言可以折獄者其由也與。子路無宿諾。

（13）　子曰聽訟吾猶人也必也使無訟乎。

（14）　子張問政子曰居之無倦行之以忠。

（15）　子曰君子成人之美不成人之惡小人反是。

（16）　季康子問政於孔子孔子對曰政者正也子帥以正孰
敢不正。

（17）　季康子患盜問於孔子孔子對曰苟子之不欲雖賞之
不竊。

（18）　季康子問政於孔子曰如殺無道以就有道何如。孔
子對曰子爲政焉用殺子欲善而民善矣君子之德風小人之
德草草上之風必偃。

（19）　子張問士何如斯可謂之達矣。子曰何哉爾所謂達

者。子張對曰在邦必聞在家必聞。子曰是聞也非達也夫達也者質直而好義察言而觀色慮以下人在邦必達在家必達。夫聞也者色取仁而行違居之不疑在邦必聞在家必聞。

(20) 樊遲從遊於舞雩之下曰敢問崇德修慝辨惑。子曰善哉問先事後得非崇德與攻其惡無攻人之惡非修慝與一朝之忿忘其身以及其親非惑與。

(21) 樊遲問仁子曰愛人問知子曰知人。樊遲未達子曰舉直錯諸枉能使枉者直。樊遲退見子夏曰鄉也吾見於夫子而問知子曰舉直錯諸枉能使枉者直何謂也。子夏曰富哉言乎舜有天下選於眾舉皐陶不仁者遠矣湯有天下選於眾舉伊尹不仁者遠矣。

(22) 子貢問友子曰忠告而善道之不可則止無自辱焉。

(23) 曾子曰君子以文會友以友輔仁。


# 十三. 子　路

（１） 子路問政子曰先之勞之。請益曰無倦。

（２） 仲弓爲季氏宰問政子曰先有司赦小過舉賢才。曰焉知賢才而舉之。曰舉爾所知爾所不知人其舍諸。

（３） 子路曰衛君待子而爲政子將奚先。子曰必也正名

乎。子路曰有是哉子之迂也奚其正。子曰野哉由也君子
於其所不知蓋闕如也名不正則言不順言不順則事不成事
不成則禮樂不興禮樂不興則刑罰不中刑罰不中則民無所
措手足。故君子名之必可言也言之必可行也君子於其言
無所苟而已矣。

（4） 樊遲請學稼子曰吾不如老農請學爲圃曰吾不如老
圃。樊遲出子曰小人哉樊須也。上好禮則民莫敢不敬上
好義則民莫敢不服上好信則民莫敢不用情夫如是則四方
之民襁負其子而至矣焉用稼。

（5） 子曰誦詩三百授之以政不達使於四方不能專對雖
多亦奚以爲。

（6） 子曰其身正不令而行其身不正雖令不從。

（7） 子曰魯衞之政兄弟也。

（8） 子謂衞公子荆善居室始有曰苟合矣少有曰苟完矣
富有曰苟美矣。

（9） 子適衞冉有僕子曰庶矣哉冉有曰旣庶矣又何加焉
曰富之。曰旣富矣又何加焉曰敎之。

（10） 子曰苟有用我者朞月而已可也三年有成。

（11） 子曰善人爲邦百年亦可以勝殘去殺矣誠哉是言也。

**（12）** 子曰如有王者必世而後仁。

(13) 子曰苟正其身矣於從政乎何有不能正其身如正人何。

(14) 冉有退朝子曰何晏也對曰有政子曰其事也如有政雖不吾以吾其與聞之。

(15) 定公問一言而可以興邦有諸。孔子對曰言不可以若是其幾也人之言曰爲君難爲臣不易如知爲君之難也不幾乎一言而興邦乎。曰一言而喪邦有諸孔子對曰言不可以若是其幾也人之言曰予無樂乎爲君唯其言而莫予違也如其善而莫之違也不亦善乎如不善而莫之違也不幾乎一言而喪邦乎。

(16) 葉公問政子曰近者說遠者來。

(17) 子夏爲莒父宰問政子曰無欲速無見小利欲速則不達見小利則大事不成。

(18) 葉公語孔子曰吾黨有直躬者其父攘羊而子證之。孔子曰 吾黨之直者 異於是 父爲子隱 子爲父隱直在其中矣。

(19) 樊遲問仁子曰居處恭執事敬與人忠雖之夷狄不可棄也。

(20) 子貢問曰何如斯可謂之士矣子曰行己有恥使於四方不辱君命可謂士矣。曰敢問其次曰宗族稱孝焉鄉黨稱弟焉。曰敢問其次曰言必信行必果硜硜然小人哉抑亦可以爲次矣。曰今之從政者何如子曰噫斗筲之人何足算也。

(21)　子曰不得中行而與之必也狂狷乎狂者進取狷者有所不爲也。

(22)　子曰南人有言曰人而無恒不可以作巫醫善夫不恒其德或承之羞。子曰不占而已矣。

(23)　子曰君子和而不同小人同而不和。

(24)　子貢問曰鄉人皆好之何如子曰未可也鄉人皆惡之何如子曰未可也不如鄉人之善者好之其不善者惡之。

(25)　子曰君子易事而難說也說之不以道不說也及其使人也器之小人難事而易說也說之雖不以道說也及其使人也求備焉。

(26)　子曰君子泰而不驕小人驕而不泰。

(27)　子曰剛毅木訥近仁。

(28)　子路問曰何如斯可謂之士矣子曰切切偲偲怡怡如也可謂士矣朋友切切偲偲兄弟怡怡。

(29)　子曰善人教民七年亦可以即戎矣。

(30)　子曰以不教民戰是謂棄之。

## 十四．憲　問

（1）　憲問恥子曰邦有道穀邦無道穀恥也。

（2）　克伐怨欲不行焉可以爲仁矣子曰可以爲難矣仁則吾不知也。

（3）　子曰士而懷居不足以爲士矣。

（4）　子曰邦有道危言危行邦無道危行言孫。

（5）　子曰有德者必有言有言者不必有德仁者必有勇勇者不必有仁。

（6）　南宮适問於孔子曰羿善射奡盪舟俱不得其死然禹稷躬稼而有天下夫子不答南宮适出子曰君子哉若人尚德哉若人。

（7）　子曰君子而不仁者有矣夫未有小人而仁者也。

（8）　子曰愛之能勿勞乎忠焉能勿誨乎。

（9）　子曰爲命裨諶草創之世叔討論之行人子羽修飾之東里子產潤色之。

（10）　或問子產子曰惠人也。問子西曰彼哉彼哉。問管仲曰人也奪伯氏駢邑三百飯疏食沒齒無怨言。

（11）　子曰貧而無怨難富而無驕易。

（12）　子曰孟公綽爲趙魏老則優不可以爲滕薛大夫。

(13)　子路問成人子曰若臧武仲之知公綽之不欲卞莊子之勇冉求之藝文之以禮樂亦可以爲成人矣。曰今之成人者何必然見利思義見危授命久要不忘平生之言亦可以爲成人矣。

(14)　子問公叔文子於公明賈曰信乎夫子不言不笑不取乎。公明賈對曰以告者過也夫子時然後言人不厭其言樂然後笑人不厭其笑義然後取人不厭其取子曰其然豈其然乎。

(15)　子曰臧武仲以防求爲後於魯雖曰不要君吾不信也。

(16)　子曰晉文公譎而不正齊桓公正而不譎。

(17)　子路曰桓公殺公子糾召忽死之管仲不死曰未仁乎。子曰桓公九合諸侯不以兵車管仲之力也如其仁如其仁。

(18)　子貢曰管仲非仁者與桓公殺公子糾不能死又相之。子曰管仲相桓公霸諸侯一匡天下民到于今受其賜微管仲吾其被髮左衽矣豈若匹夫匹婦之爲諒也自經於溝瀆而莫之知也。

(19)　公叔文子之臣大夫僎與文子同升諸公子聞之曰可以爲文矣。

(20)　子言衛靈公之無道也康子曰夫如是奚而不喪。孔子曰仲叔圉治賓客祝鮀治宗廟王孫賈治軍旅夫如是奚其喪。

(21) 子曰其言之不怍則爲之也難。

(22) 陳成子弒簡公。孔子沐浴而朝告於哀公曰陳恒弒其君請討之公曰告夫三子。孔子曰以吾從大夫之後不敢不告也君曰告夫三子者。之三子告不可孔子曰以吾從大夫之後不敢不告也。

(23) 子路問事君子曰勿欺也而犯之。

(24) 子曰君子上達小人下達。

(25) 子曰古之學者爲己今之學者爲人。

(26) 蘧伯玉使人於孔子孔子與之坐而問焉曰夫子何爲對曰夫子欲寡其過而未能也使者出子曰使乎使乎。

(27) 曾子曰君子思不出其位。

(28) 子曰君子恥其言而過其行。

(29) 子曰君子道者三我無能焉仁者不憂知者不惑勇者不懼。子貢曰夫子自道也。

(30) 子貢方人子曰賜也賢乎哉夫我則不暇。

(31) 子曰不患人之不己知患其不能也。

(32) 子曰不逆詐不億不信抑亦先覺者是賢乎。

(33) 微生畝謂孔子曰丘何爲是栖栖者與無乃爲佞乎。孔子曰非敢爲佞也疾固也。

(34) 子曰驥不稱其力稱其德也。

（35）　或曰以德報怨何如。子曰何以報德以直報怨以德報德。

（36）　子曰莫我知也夫子貢曰何為其莫知子也子曰不怨天不尤人下學而上達知我者其天乎。

（37）　公伯寮愬子路於季孫子服景伯以告曰夫子固有惑志於公伯寮吾力猶能肆諸市朝子曰道之將行也與命也道之將廢也與命也公伯寮其如命何。

（38）　子曰賢者辟世其次辟地其次辟色其次辟言。

（39）　子曰作者七人矣。

（40）　子路宿於石門晨門曰奚自子路曰自孔氏曰是知其不可而為之者與。

（41）　子擊磬於衛有荷蕢而過孔氏之門者曰有心哉擊磬乎既而曰鄙哉硜硜乎莫己知也斯已而已矣深則厲淺則揭。子曰果哉末之難矣。

（42）　子張曰書云高宗諒陰三年不言何謂也。子曰何必高宗古之人皆然君薨百官總己以聽於冢宰三年。

（43）　子曰上好禮則民易使也。

（44）　子路問君子子曰修己以敬曰如斯而已乎曰修己以安人曰如斯而已乎曰修己以安百姓修己以安百姓堯舜其猶病諸。

（45） 原壤夷俟子曰幼而不孫弟長而無述焉老而不死是
爲賊以杖叩其脛。

（46） 闕黨童子將命或問之曰益者與子曰吾見其居於位
也見其與先生並行也非求益者也欲速成者也。

## 十五. 衛 靈 公

（1） 衛靈公問陳於孔子孔子對曰俎豆之事則嘗聞之矣
軍旅之事未之學也明日遂行。在陳絕糧從者病莫能興子
路慍見曰君子亦有窮乎子曰君子固窮小人窮斯濫矣。

（2） 子曰賜也女以予爲多學而識之者與對曰然非與曰
非也予一以貫之。子曰由知德者鮮矣。

（3） 子曰無爲而治者其舜也與夫何爲哉恭己正南面而
已矣。

（4） 子張問行子曰言忠信行篤敬雖蠻貊之邦行矣言不
忠信行不篤敬雖州里行乎哉。立則見其參於前也在輿則
見其倚於衡也夫然後行。子張書諸紳。

（5） 子曰直哉史魚邦有道如矢邦無道如矢。君子哉蘧
伯玉邦有道則仕邦無道則可卷而懷之。

（6） 子曰可與言而不與之言失人不可與言而與之言失

昌知者不失人亦不失言。

（7）　子曰志士仁人無求生以害仁有殺身以成仁。

（8）　子貢問為仁子曰工欲善其事必先利其器居是邦也事其大夫之賢者友其士之仁者。

（9）　顏淵問為邦子曰行夏之時乘殷之輅服周之冕樂則韶舞放鄭聲遠佞人鄭聲淫佞人殆。

（10）　子曰人無遠慮必有近憂。

（11）　子曰已矣乎吾未見好德如好色者也。

（12）　子曰臧文仲其竊位者與知柳下惠之賢而不與立也。

（13）　子曰躬自厚而薄責於人則遠怨矣。

（14）　子曰不曰如之何如之何者吾末如之何也已矣。

（15）　子曰羣居終日言不及義好行小慧難矣哉。

（16）　子曰君子義以為質禮以行之孫以出之信以成之君子哉。

（17）　子曰君子病無能焉不病人之不己知也。

（18）　子曰君子疾沒世而名不稱焉。

（19）　子曰君子求諸己小人求諸人。

（20）　子曰君子矜而不爭羣而不黨。

（21）　子曰君子不以言舉人不以人廢言。

（22）　子貢問曰有一言而可以終身行之者乎子曰其恕乎

己所不欲勿施於人。

(23)　子曰吾之於人也誰毀誰譽如有所譽者其有所試矣。
斯民也三代之所以直道而行也。

(24)　子曰吾猶及史之闕文也有馬者借人乘之今亡已夫。

(25)　子曰巧言亂德小不忍則亂大謀。

(26)　子曰衆惡之必察焉衆好之必察焉。

(27)　子曰人能弘道非道弘人。

(28)　子曰過而不改是謂過矣。

(29)　子曰吾嘗終日不食終夜不寢以思無益不如學也。

(30)　子曰君子謀道不謀食耕也餒在其中矣學也祿在其
中矣君子憂道不憂貧。

(31)　子曰知及之仁不能守之雖得之必失之。知及之仁
能守之不莊以涖之則民不敬。知及之仁能守之莊以涖之
動之不以禮未善也。

(32)　子曰君子不可小知而可大受也小人不可大受而可
小知也。

(33)　子曰民之於仁也甚於水火水火吾見蹈而死者矣未
見蹈仁而死者也。

(34)　子曰當仁不讓於師。

**(35)　子曰君子貞而不諒。**

（36）　子曰事君敬其事而後其食。

（37）　子曰有教無類。

（38）　子曰道不同不相爲謀。

（39）　子曰辭達而已矣。

（40）　師冕見及階子曰階也及席子曰席也皆坐子告之曰某在斯某在斯。師冕出子張問曰與師言之道與子曰然固相師之道也。


## 十六. 季　氏

（1）　季氏將伐顓臾。冉有季路見於孔子曰季氏將有事於顓臾。孔子曰求無乃爾是過與。夫顓臾昔者先王以爲東蒙主且在邦域之中矣是社稷之臣也何以伐爲。冉有曰夫子欲之吾二臣者皆不欲也。孔子曰求周任有言曰陳力就列不能者止危而不持顛而不扶則將焉用彼相矣。且爾言過矣虎兕出於柙龜玉毀於櫝中是誰之過與。冉有曰今夫顓臾固而近於費今不取後世必爲子孫憂。孔子曰求君子疾夫舍曰欲之而必爲之辭。丘也聞有國有家者不患寡而患不均不患貧而患不安蓋均無貧和無寡安無傾。夫如是故遠人不服則修文德以來之既來之則安之。今由與求

也相夫子遠人不服而不能來也邦分崩離析而不能守也而
謀動干戈於邦內吾恐季孫之憂不在顓臾而在蕭牆之內也。

（2）　孔子曰天下有道則禮樂征伐自天子出天下無道則
禮樂征伐自諸侯出自諸侯出蓋十世希不失矣自大夫出五
世希不失矣陪臣執國命三世希不失矣。天下有道則政不
在大夫天下有道則庶人不議。

（3）　孔子曰祿之去公室五世矣政逮於大夫四世矣故夫
三桓之子孫微矣。

（4）　孔子曰益者三友損者三友友直友諒友多聞益矣友
便辟友善柔友便佞損矣。

（5）　孔子曰益者三樂損者三樂樂節禮樂樂道人之善樂
多賢友益矣樂驕樂樂佚遊樂宴樂損矣。

（6）　孔子曰侍於君子有三愆言未及之而言謂之躁言及
之而不言謂之隱未見顏色而言謂之瞽。

（7）　孔子曰君子有三戒少之時血氣未定戒之在色及其
壯也血氣方剛戒之在鬭及其老也血氣既衰戒之在得。

（8）　孔子曰君子有三畏畏天命畏大人畏聖人之言小人
不知天命而不畏也狎大人侮聖人之言。

（9）　孔子曰生而知之者上也學而知之者次也困而學之
又其次也困而不學民斯為下矣。

(10)　孔子曰君子有九思視思明聽思聰色思溫貌思恭言
思忠事思敬疑思問忿思難見得思義。

(11)　孔子曰見善如不及見不善如探湯吾見其人矣吾聞
其語矣。隱居以求其志行義以達其道吾聞其語矣未見其
人也。

(12)　齊景公有馬千駟死之日民無得而稱焉伯夷叔齊餓
於首陽之下民到于今稱之誠不以富亦祇以異其斯之謂與。

(13)　陳亢問於伯魚曰子亦有異聞乎對曰未也嘗獨立鯉
趨而過庭曰學詩乎對曰未也不學詩無以言鯉退而學詩。
他日又獨立鯉趨而過庭曰學禮乎對曰未也不學禮無以立
鯉退而學禮聞斯二者。陳亢退而喜曰問一得三聞詩聞禮
又聞君子之遠其子也。

(14)　邦君之妻君稱之曰夫人夫人自稱曰小童邦人稱之
曰君夫人稱諸異邦曰寡小君異邦人稱之亦曰君夫人。

# 十七　陽　貨

（1）　陽貨欲見孔子孔子不見歸孔子豚孔子時其亡也而
往拜之遇諸塗。謂孔子曰來予與爾言曰懷其寶而迷其邦
可謂仁乎曰不可好從事而亟失時可謂知乎曰不可日月逝

矣歲不我與孔子曰諾吾將仕矣。

（2）　子曰性相近也習相遠也。

（3）　子曰唯上知與下愚不移。

（4）　子之武城聞絃歌之聲夫子莞爾而笑曰割雞焉用牛刀。子游對曰昔者偃也聞諸夫子曰君子學道則愛人小人學道則易使也。子曰二三子偃之言是也前言戲之耳。

（5）　公山弗擾以費畔召子欲往子路不說曰末之也已何必公山氏之之也。子曰夫召我者而豈徒哉如有用我者吾其爲東周乎。

（6）　子張問仁於孔子孔子曰能行五者於天下爲仁矣請問之曰恭寬信敏惠恭則不侮寬則得衆信則人任焉敏則有功惠則足以使人。

（7）　佛肸召子欲往子路曰昔者由也聞諸夫子曰親於其身爲不善者君子不入也佛肸以中牟畔子之往也如之何。子曰然有是言也不曰堅乎磨而不磷不曰白乎涅而不緇吾豈匏瓜也哉焉能繫而不食。

（8）　子曰由也女聞六言六蔽矣乎對曰未也。居吾語女好仁不好學其蔽也愚好知不好學其蔽也蕩好信不好學其蔽也賊好直不好學其蔽也絞好勇不好學其蔽也亂好剛不好學其蔽也狂。

（9）　子曰小子何莫學夫詩詩可以興可以觀可以羣可以
怨邇之事父遠之事君多識於鳥獸草木之名。

（10）　子謂伯魚曰女爲周南召南矣乎人而不爲周南召南
其猶正牆面而立也與。

（11）　子曰禮云禮云玉帛云乎哉樂云樂云鍾鼓云乎哉。

（12）　子曰色厲而內荏譬諸小人其猶穿窬之盜也與。

（13）　子曰鄉原德之賊也。

（14）　子曰道聽而塗說德之棄也。

（15）　子曰鄙夫可與事君也與哉其未得之也患得之既得
之患失之苟患失之無所不至矣。

（16）　子曰古者民有三疾今也或是之亡也古之狂也肆今
之狂也蕩古之矜也廉今之矜也忿戾古之愚也直今之愚也
詐而已矣。

（17）　子曰惡紫之奪朱也惡鄭聲之亂雅樂也惡利口之覆
邦家者。

（18）　子曰予欲無言子貢曰子如不言則小子何述焉子曰
天何言哉四時行焉百物生焉天何言哉。

（19）　孺悲欲見孔子孔子辭以疾將命者出戶取瑟而歌使
之聞之。

（20）　宰我問三年之喪期已久矣君子三年不爲禮禮必壞

三年不爲樂樂必崩舊穀旣沒新穀旣升鑽燧改火期可已矣。

子曰食夫稻衣夫錦於女安乎曰安女安則爲之夫君子之居喪食旨不甘聞樂不樂居處不安故不爲也今女安則爲之。

宰我出子曰予之不仁也子生三年然後免於父母之懷夫三年之喪天下之通喪也予也有三年之愛於其父母乎。

(21) 子曰飽食終日無所用心難矣哉不有博奕者乎爲之猶賢乎已。

(22) 子路曰君子尙勇乎子曰君子義以爲上君子有勇而無義爲亂小人有勇而無義爲盜。

(23) 子貢曰君子亦有惡乎子曰有惡惡稱人之惡者惡居下流而訕上者惡勇而無禮者惡果敢而窒者。曰賜也亦有惡乎惡徼以爲知者惡不孫以爲勇者惡訐以爲直者。

(24) 子曰唯女子與小人爲難養也近之則不孫遠之則怨。

(25) 子曰年四十而見惡焉其終也已。


## 十八. 微  子

(1) 微子去之箕子爲之奴比干諫而死。孔子曰殷有三仁焉。

(2) 柳下惠爲士師三黜人曰子未可以去乎曰直道以事人焉往而不三黜枉道以事人何必去父母之邦。

（3）　齊景公待孔子曰若季氏則吾不能以季孟之間待之曰吾老矣不能用也孔子行。

（4）　齊人歸女樂季桓子受之三日不朝孔子行。

（5）　楚狂接輿歌而過孔子曰鳳兮鳳兮何德之衰往者不可諫來者猶可追已而已而今之從政者殆而。孔子下欲與之言趨而辟之不得與之言。

（6）　長沮桀溺耦而耕孔子過之使子路問津焉。長沮曰夫執輿者為誰子路曰為孔丘曰是魯孔丘與曰是也曰是知津矣。問於桀溺桀溺曰子為誰曰仲由曰是魯孔丘之徒與對曰然曰滔滔者天下皆是也而誰以易之且而與其從辟人之士也豈若從辟世之士哉耰而不輟。子路行以告夫子憮然曰鳥獸不可與同羣吾非斯人之徒與而誰與天下有道丘不與易也。

（7）　子路從而後遇丈人以杖荷蓧子路問曰子見夫子乎丈人曰四體不勤五穀不分孰為夫子植其杖而芸。子路拱而立止子路宿殺雞為黍而食之見其二子焉。明日子路行以告子曰隱者也使子路反見之至則行矣。子路曰不仕無義長幼之節不可廢也君臣之義如之何其廢之欲潔其身而亂大倫君子之仕也行其義也道之不行已知之矣。

（8）　逸民伯夷叔齊虞仲夷逸朱張柳下惠少連。子曰不降

其志不辱其身伯夷叔齊與。謂柳下惠少連降志辱身矣言
中倫行中慮其斯而已矣。謂虞仲夷逸隱居放言身中清廢
中權。我則異於是無可無不可。

（9） 大師摯適齊亞飯干適楚三飯繚適蔡四飯缺適秦鼓
方叔入于河播鼗武入于漢少師陽擊磬襄入于海。

(10) 周公謂魯公曰君子不施其親不使大臣怨乎不以故
舊無大故則不棄也無求備於一人。

(11) 周有八士伯達伯适仲突仲忽叔夜叔夏季隨季騧。


## 十九 子　張

（1） 子張曰士見危致命見得思義祭思敬喪思哀其可已
矣。

（2） 子張曰執德不弘信道不篤焉能為有焉能為亡。

（3） 子夏之門人問交於子夏子張曰子夏云何對曰子夏
曰可者與之其不可者拒之子張曰異乎吾所聞君子尊賢而
容眾嘉善而矜不能我之大賢與於人何所不容我之不賢與
人將拒我如之何其拒人也。

（4） 子夏曰雖小道必有可觀者焉致遠恐泥是以君子不
為也。

（5） 子夏曰日知其所亡月無忘其所能可謂好學也已矣。

（6）　子夏曰博學而篤志切問而近思仁在其中矣。

（7）　子夏曰百工居肆以成其事君子學以致其道。

（8）　子夏曰小人之過也必文。

（9）　子夏曰君子有三變望之儼然即之也溫聽其言也厲。

（10）　子夏曰君子信而後勞其民未信則以爲厲己也信而後諫未信則以爲謗己也。

（11）　子夏曰大德不踰閑小德出入可也。

（12）　子游曰子夏之門人小子當灑掃應對進退則可矣抑末也本之則無如之何。子夏聞之曰噫言游過矣君子之道孰先傳焉孰後倦焉譬諸草木區以別矣君子之道焉可誣也有始有卒者其惟聖人乎。

（13）　子夏曰仕而優則學學而優則仕。

（14）　子游曰喪致乎哀而止。

（15）　子游曰吾友張也爲難能也然而未仁。

（16）　曾子曰堂堂乎張也難與並爲仁矣。

（17）　曾子曰吾聞諸夫子人未有自致者也必也親喪乎。

（18）　曾子曰吾聞諸夫子孟莊子之孝也其他可能也其不改父之臣與父之政是難能也。

（19）　孟氏使陽膚爲士師問於曾子曾子曰上失其道民散久矣如得其情則哀矜而勿喜。

(20)　子貢曰紂之不善不如是之甚也是以君子惡居下流天下之惡皆歸焉。

(21)　子貢曰君子之過也如日月之食焉過也人皆見之更也人皆仰之。

(22)　衛公孫朝問於子貢曰仲尼焉學子貢曰文武之道未墜於地在人賢者識其大者不賢者識其小者莫不有文武之道焉夫子焉不學而亦何常師之有。

(23)　叔孫武叔語大夫於朝曰子貢賢於仲尼子服景伯以告子貢子貢曰譬之宮牆賜之牆也及肩窺見室家之好夫子之牆數仞不得其門而入不見宗廟之美百官之富得其門者或寡矣夫子之云不亦宜乎。

(24)　叔孫武叔毀仲尼子貢曰無以為也仲尼不可毀也他人之賢者丘陵也猶可踰也仲尼日月也無得而踰焉人雖欲自絕其何傷於日月乎多見其不知量也。

(25)　陳子禽謂子貢曰子為恭也仲尼豈賢於子乎子貢曰君子一言以為知一言以為不知言不可不慎也。夫子之不可及也猶天之不可階而升也。夫子之得邦家者所謂立之斯道之斯行綏之斯來動之斯和其生也榮其死也哀如之何其可及也。

## 二十. 堯　曰

（1）　堯曰咨爾舜天之曆數在爾躬允執其中四海困窮天
祿永終。舜亦以命禹。曰予小子履敢用玄牡敢昭告于皇
皇后帝有罪不敢赦帝臣不蔽簡在帝心朕躬有罪無以萬方
萬方有罪罪在朕躬。周有大賚善人是富。雖有周親不如
仁人百姓有過在予一人。謹權量審法度修廢官四方之政
行焉。興滅國繼絕世舉逸民天下之民歸心焉。所重民食
喪祭。寬則得衆信則民任焉敏則有功公則說。

（2）　子張問於孔子曰何如斯可以從政矣子曰尊五美屏
四惡斯可以從政矣子張曰何謂五美子曰君子惠而不費勞
而不怨欲而不貪泰而不驕威而不猛子張曰何謂惠而不費
子曰因民之所利而利之斯不亦惠而不費乎擇可勞而勞之
又誰怨欲仁而得仁又焉貪君子無衆寡無小大無敢慢斯不
亦泰而不驕乎君子正其衣冠尊其瞻視儼然人望而畏之斯
不亦威而不猛乎子張曰何謂四惡子曰不教而殺謂之虐
不戒視成謂之暴慢令致期謂之賊猶之與人也出納之吝謂
之有司。

（3）　子曰不知命無以為君子也不知禮無以立也不知言
無以知人也。

**英譯論語**　　　　　　定價 150원

1960年　12月 1日　　初版發行
1962年　4月 30日　　再版發行

譯　者　卞　榮　泰
發行者　李　炳　俊
發行處　民　衆　書　舘
刷印處　民衆書舘工務局